Seaside day out – a special treat in the 1930s

So Far So Good
Memoir of a Croydon Girl in the Roaring 20s

© Freda Beaven 2017

All rights reserved

The moral right of the author has been asserted

No part of this book may be reproduced or transmitted in any form or by any means without permission, except by a reviewer who wishes to quote brief passages in connection with a review written for insertion in a newspaper, magazine or broadcast.

All photographs from the Author's private collection

The name Clutterbuck is of uncertain origin but is possibly from a family from Belgium/Freesia/Netherlands in the 16th century, spelt Clotterbooke in one record then.

There has long been trade between the West Country of Britain and the Flemings and there were anti-Flemish riots during the Peasants' Revolt of 1381.

Entries in Burke's Landed Gentry 18th Edition Vol. III trace the family from c.1550 occupation Broadweavers, no doubt a flourishing business at that time. A connection with Belgium is mentioned by Chaucer in Canterbury Tales where he says of the Wife of Bath –

> *'At clooth makying she hadẹ swich an haunt*
>
> *She passẹd hem of Ypres and of Gaunt'*

which is understood to mean that she was such a good manufacturer that she surpassed the Flemish (who dominated the trade)

What follows is my recollection of my life, born Freda Margaret Goldsmith in Croydon, July 1923.

Contents

Acknowledgments 5
So Far So Good 7
Picture Gallery 1 23
Sid and Annie 25
The First Eight Years 34
A New House 47
Changes 60
Heading for the War Years 70
Back to Croydon 79
Moving On 88
Australia and Afterwards 97
Gathering Momentum 104
From South to North 119
Picture Gallery 2 132
The Austrian Holiday 138
Retirement 148

Acknowledgments

Having had to make my own path in many ways, my vivid memories are of kindness and help when needed, love, laughter and encouragement in abundance. My thanks, therefore, radiate in all directions where our paths have crossed. As the years advance, chances to meet past acquaintances and enjoy time together grow fewer.

However, throughout the last twenty-seven years, one constant has been my weekly visit to Lynn's Hairstylists where Jean and Lesley have cared for and styled my head of hair – something I cannot do for myself. So a big thank you goes to them, and to other dear people there who make my Thursday mornings shine with their friendship and help. Thanks also must go to my Doctor and staff at my local surgery for their invaluable care and attention.

Without a doubt, enormous thanks must go to my great friend Becky Tallentire, without whose enduring love, patience and enthusiasm this book would not have reached publication. Becky is always at hand, watching over me, supplying needs, and generally caring. She is a beautiful person; strong, tall, elegant and slim, expert at many things, especially changing light bulbs. And of course, Becky is much cleverer on the internet than I am.

So Far So Good

My Grandparents Frank and Fanny Clutterbuck

Inspired by Alan Bennett's delightful book, *The Uncommon Reader*, I would like to put on record a few things which have occurred throughout my life which may be of interest to someone, and in so doing use my voice to speak where I have not before spoken.

Family history research which I have done and written about elsewhere, took me back as far as 1733 when

Sarah, wife of Luke Clutterbuck, was born. These two people were married in Rodborough, Gloucestershire. There are still a fair number of Clutterbucks in that area. The records led me through to my maternal grandfather Frank James Clutterbuck who was to become a strong influence in my life.

In due course Frank married Fanny Odell on 3rd April 1887 at Croydon Parish Church. Fanny's mother was a Nicholson before marrying Walter Odell. Grandfather (he disliked being called Granddad and I agree with him – as I find I often do) talked to me and listened. I remember when I was about six years old being lifted on to his knee on his big Windsor kitchen chair, to recite my letters and numbers. In later life I would walk around his beautiful walled garden with him, admiring his plants; he was a passionate gardener and I was so thrilled when he cut and gave me one of his special roses.

In their youth, they were both quite tall, Fanny had flaxen hair which stayed that way all her life and she wore taken up into a cottage-loaf style. She had a beautiful face which my cousin Muriel and I remarked upon to her one day; never a wrinkle, in spite of a life as full of bad and good happenings as anybody else's. I seem to have inherited her lack of wrinkles but cannot think of any of her female descendants who have flaxen hair. I think that passed to my cousins Roger and David.

Grandfather once told me how her lovely hair hung down her back and how he chased her round lampposts during their courting days. Once he asked me if I could play a song for him on his piano. Of course I could. It was *'Genevieve, Sweet Genevieve'* and he sang along with it. I can see the scene and hear him now. The music was in my head and it was no problem for me to produce it. This was at their last house, Mavis Bank, 31 Howard Road, Woodside Green, Croydon, which also had a walled garden and Grandma raised houseplants in the conservatory.

Frank and Fanny had several house moves in their married life as their family increased. The first baby arrived in January 1888 and was named Ethel Susannah. Next was Florence Bertha, born in September 1889, then in July 1891 the twins arrived, Annie (my mother) at 6 a.m. and Grace an hour later. In February 1893 Edith was born, followed by Louisa Frances in May 1895, William James in May

1897, Doris Ruth (known as Ruth in later years) in January 1903 and Leonard Walter in October 1912.

These were my aunts and uncles, much involved with my early life. I was often told that Edith was born between Florence and the twins and one of my mother's elderly cousins told me she remembered that Edith used to push the twins in their pram. I have all their birth certificates and these tell me that Edith was born after the twins.

Strange confusion.

Florence, Annie (my mother), Edith, Doris, Grace, Ethel, Daisy (bride's mother) and Louisa at the wedding of Douglas and Hilda

By the time I knew them, these grandparents lived in the elegant house known as Laurel Villa, 93 St. James' Road, Croydon. This has now been modernised with little respect for its original character. When I knew it there were front iron railings and a front gate into a small garden area where the laurels grew, stone steps up to a heavy front door with coloured glass panels. There was a breakfast room on the lowest level and a large family kitchen and scullery, and a basement. On the entrance hall level was the big sitting room, much used for family gatherings, a large bedroom, lavatory and exit through a picture-glass panelled door, down steps to the big walled garden.

The floor above contained sizeable rooms which became a self-contained apartment, and above that similar rooms, built for staff, were let out as a small flat. The house had originally been bought by my great grandfather. It would have been well filled with seven girls, two sons, parents and visitors.

Visiting was very much a social thing to do; Grandma was 'at home' each afternoon when work was finished and expected her grown-up children to return to the bosom of the family as often as possible. A prized possession of mine is a set of eight DVD produced from the BBC's production of John Galsworthy's *'The Forsyte Saga'*, about 24 episodes. Apart from it being a magnificent story, I can see my own family customs in it, ignoring the different wealth levels and the fact that those characters inhabited Park Lane and the Bayswater Road! The Saga researches Victorian and Edwardian times and goes right through into my own early childhood.

My Grandparents' house at 93 St James' Road, Croydon

Most of the houses in which the Clutterbuck children were born (maybe not the actual buildings but at least the location) I have traced and photographed, but Leonard's birthplace has long gone. One was in Eridge Road but that no longer exists in name although we can look along the road where it was, near Mayday Road.

Mother said that as children they used to play outside in the road if it was clear, but would scamper indoors if their father appeared round the corner, as he disapproved. This brings me again to my grandfather (do I have a fixation?); whenever the adults mentioned him I heard, *'he was a difficult man'*. It does seem to me that this might be an unfair reputation. I believe he suffered a nervous breakdown and at some time must have seemed at odds with his situation, but until his son William was grown to manhood he was the lone male amongst eight women. A touch frustrating, I think.

Frank did not like to have his flowers picked but preferred to see them growing as he had set them in place. That didn't stop Fanny from letting the girls pick some to take home, saying, "Father won't know". Of course he knew. I know that he adored his wife and children and wanted them to do well in life. When he died he left £100 to each of them, with Leonard's share to go to William for the care of Leonard.

Although my grandparents married at Croydon Parish Church, the family thereafter always attended West Croydon Baptist Church, known as Spurgeon's Tabernacle. The pastor there was a young Reverend Eustace Victor Whittle. In Grandfather's later years he did not attend church very often but read his Bible at home. He disliked being preached at by a younger man and had his own beliefs and disbeliefs. Also he had rheumatic joints which made sitting on hard pews very painful. He wore Thermogene next to his skin, which, it cannot be denied, has a distinctive medicinal odour, so it may have been a relief to people who sat near to him when he ceased to attend. The family pew was in the gallery of the tabernacle, to the left as you face the choir.

I became aware of my aunts and uncles when they were past their teens and adult. Aunt Ethel, the eldest, was tall and rather solemn in character, very kind-hearted and caring. I don't know what work she did or training she may have had. My mother did tell me that Ethel once was absent from home for several days and nights; nobody knew where she was. What a mystery.

Ethel married George Main and they produced Gordon, Joyce, Doris and Ruby. Auntie Flo was tall and trained as a tailoress, becoming professional at the skill which she used well in later life. She married Frederick, step-brother of my Grandfather, thus an uncle to Flo and she retained her own family name. As such a marriage was illegal in our country, Fred went to America where Flo joined him and they married there. They lived in California and had no children. Auntie Grace, I believe had tailoring training but did not follow the profession after marrying Herbert Jones in 1924, a widower who had three children, Richard (Dick), Ronald and Muriel. They went to live in Guildford, Surrey.

My mother went into service as a cook/housemaid. She became very unhappy working under a cook who was prone to drinking, so Grandfather let her come home as he would not have his family miserable in their situations. I don't know if Aunt Edith had training but she set up as a milliner and opened a shop on Spurgeon's Bridge. Edith was adventurous and full of ideas. She married Arthur

Sayer in New Zealand and opened a hat shop in Auckland, calling it *Edith of Bond Street* – not saying which Bond Street. It became highly successful.

There were frequent letters home from New Zealand but the family couldn't find out what was Arthur's occupation there. Edith wrote that he worked for the government. The sisters assumed that meant he was a prison officer. He was a tall man with military bearing and had been a guardsman in London, as they well knew. In recent years, information and photos which I now have, show him to have been of considerable consequence in New Zealand, both he and Edith were included in royal functions.

When these aunts were children, milk was delivered from a cart in the street; you took your jug to the cart and it was filled from a tap. Edith was the one who once mischievously turned the tap down and they all ran away.

The twins were identical and remained so into later life. Grace was the dominant one and Annie followed along, more or less. They were closely bonded and often had similar thoughts and experiences though miles apart.

Louisa – Auntie Lou – was also intrigued by hats but mostly of the bought kind. I don't know if she made any but she certainly wore them well. I found her always pleasant and entertaining. She was a fair pianist and could rattle through *'The Robin's Return'* with aplomb. The older sisters often found her irritating and a bit of a butterfly; she reminded me of the character Amy in Louisa Alcott's *'Little Women'*. Louie married Harold Dowley and their children were Joy, Maurice and Dennis.

Uncle Will was the first-born son whose arrival must have been quite a thrill. He was in the army during the 1914-1918 war; Mother said they heard his footsteps on the stairs as he sometimes stumbled to bed after being out with his army pals. Will married Daisy Allen and they first had a daughter, Hilda, then 10 years later a son, David.

I remember they lived in a house on London Road, Thornton Heath, and eventually moved to Richmond Road. Auntie Daisy made for me a kimono which I was to wear in a school tableau of different countries. The material was heavy brocade and there was a wide sash and enormous pocket sleeves, Japanese style. It was lovely. Also when I was ten years old she made me a bridesmaid's dress of pink material which thrilled me. This was for the wedding of Dick Jones and Dorothy Faulkner at Guildford. I wore it all day Christmas Day that year. Muriel and I were two of four bridesmaids for Dorothy.

The last of the daughters to arrive was Doris Ruth who, as she grew into her 20s, welcomed the new generation of post-war ideas. She grew tall, slender and very pretty, lively and modern-minded. Her first job that I knew about was with the local electricity board as a demonstrator of the new home appliances. So Grandma and the sisters began to acquire cookers, Servis washing machines, irons etc., all fuelled by electricity. These early washing machines consisted of a circular tub to contain water and the items to be washed, supported on a sturdy frame, a tap to drain the used water, and above were two rubber rollers on a swivel, to squeeze out the water – considered a great advance on the old mangle. What a pity it came to Grandma when all her children were grown up and doing their own washing.

Doris lived with her friend, Ruby Armitage in the self-contained apartment at No. 93. Ruby appeared, I know not when, from a well-to-do family at Guildford, where she had a sister named Ursula. She probably belonged to a Society of Do-Good ladies, but I never knew exactly who they were. Her working dress was something like that of a nun but she was not a catholic. Her time was spent in Croydon's poor area around Wilford Road, administering to women whose husbands were mostly employed (or unemployed) by the local bell foundry, Gillett & Johnson. Auntie Ruby was a welcome addition to my own life as I remember. Ruby and Doris sang in the choir pews at Spurgeon's, the family church. Doris married Herbert Norman Nunn and a son, Roger, was born to them.

When Grandma was 45 years old, Leonard Walter was born. Sadly he was found to have learning difficulties. There was no thought in those days of him being encouraged to read and write. We might have called him autistic today. He was adored and lovingly cared for by my grandparents who would not ever consider him being 'put away'. He had amazing skills in some ways.

Early in the 1930s they moved to Woodside Green and one prized possession was a record player in a handsome cabinet. Leonard amused himself for hours putting on records and he would correctly put on and play any one for which we asked. He had his own way of recognising titles. He was a lovely person, devoted to his parents and quite a good mimic. Grandfather sometimes attended a Brotherhood religious meeting, taking Leonard with him, and I have watched Len give a demonstration of the speaker (when he thought nobody was looking or listening) waving his arms about and shouting the Good News. Then he would giggle.

Grandma with her younger son, Leonard

There was a sad occasion one day when I was visiting. Also present were my mother, several aunts and chiefly, Aunt Edith on a visit home from NZ. Len was washing dishes in the kitchen. Maybe he was frightened by all the noisy excitement and wanted Grandma's attention. He didn't remember who Edith was; she'd been away for many years so what was all the fuss about? In a flash he came with scissors and stabbed his mother in the leg, not seriously but it was a scare. He had never done such a thing before and was most distressed afterwards. Someone must have contacted the local authorities and they did remove Lenny to a hospital, which caused my grandparents great grief. When they visited him he asked repeatedly for Woodside Green.

In 1943 a bomb fell on the house next door, I believe killing their neighbours, Mr and Mrs Hook. Leonard, Grandma and Grandfather all died later that year, within six weeks, and that was a very sad ending.

I have written a great deal about the Clutterbuck family because I grew up with all these aunts and uncles, plus some others who were just as important to me but perhaps not seen so often. It gives me much pleasure and comfort to think how we all knew each other as a big family. There was always someone nearby, someone we knew, could care about and include in a visiting round. My contemporary cousins and their families grew up in the same way and we spent a fair amount of time together as children. Of course, life has brought the usual share of troubles, one way and another, but most of us and our descendants are not doing too badly.

Leonard used to play a record which I remember:- *"We all have to go through the mill, you know..."*
We do, too.

Lenny with his parents.

Picture Gallery 1

Grandma with Edith (standing) and Ruby Armitage

Grandfather's sisters L-R – Amy, Bertha, Harriet and Lillian

Cousin May

Sid and Annie

Freda with Auntie Doris at the seaside

My brother Ronald used to tell the tale that in the days when my father, Sidney Goldsmith, was courting my mother, Annie Clutterbuck, there was a mix-up between the twins. He had arranged to meet Annie somewhere in Croydon, Grace turned up and confusion ensued. How it got sorted nobody seemed to know but Ron believed it was true. How different life might have been.

The Goldsmiths and the Clutterbucks were broadly in the same line of business; building and plumbing. As a small boy my Uncle Horace (my father's brother) is said to have spoken his first words, which were "Mr Clutterbuck at the door for you, Father". I find that my childhood was much less involved with the Goldsmiths, even though Grandma Goldsmith was an early visitor at my birth and noticed a problem.

My father and two of his brothers, Reginald Herbert and Horace Walter were born at Beaconsfield Road, a parallel road to where I was born, diagonally about one hundred yards away. Their later address was Pemdevon Road, Croydon, which is not listed in the 1896 Ward's Croydon Directory so was probably in a new building area. That would have been where the next family additions were born, my other Aunt Ethel, Uncle Arthur, and Lillian who died at five years old.

The earliest Goldsmiths whom I have traced were George, born in 1825, who was a blacksmith at Hellingly, and three of his brothers – Stephen who worked for the Water Board in Eastbourne, James who emigrated to Australia and Herbert who was a wheelwright at Jevington, all in Sussex. The Old Forge at Jevington can still be identified but when I was there a few years ago it had become, not surprisingly, a Post Office and General Store. Jevington was referred to in hushed tones when I was a child – family secret?

So George was my great-grandfather; he married Jane Wenham and they had ten children. Of those I knew two, Jabez James (known as J.J.) and Herbert John who became my grandfather. Some of the family came to live in Croydon and Great-Grandfather George founded an ironmongery business there, with some of his sons, which was listed in the Directory as GOLDSMITH (G) AND SONS, Ironmongers & co., 96 Whitehorse Road. It became successful and I remember it well. Herbert, however, fell out of favour with the family and could not partake of the financial fruits of this business and thus the moneyed side of the family became separated from the other (my) side. What a pity.

I don't know where they met but Herbert John married Frances Rasell. That spelling is correct according to one official document, but I think it may have been Rassell. Frances had been born in New York, America, by the Hudson River – a particularly sparse address being all that our Aunt Ethel could pass on. I have visions of a Moses basket…

A violin found in a family attic was understood to have been made by Frances' father on board ship to America and I have heard that he made a bow which he sold to pay for the family journey back to England. Many years later the violin was passed to my son Derek who was very interested in this heirloom.

Annie, the firstborn of the Clutterbuck twins became married to Sidney John Goldsmith, eldest son of Herbert John and Frances Goldsmith, on 29th October 1914 at Croydon Baptist Church on Spurgeon's Bridge. They lived immediately in a house at nearby Beddington but I think not for long, and then moved to Guildford Road, Selhurst, West Croydon, where eventually both Ronald and I were born.

I must state that whatever I now write here about my life and my immediate family is, and can only be part of whatever happened, a part of what I felt then and what I feel now. There was much that was and is good. My home was loving, warm and comfortable. My father was always employed by Hall & Company of Croydon, in a white-collar job. I remember those white collars; it was my job to collect them from the laundry where they were sent each week. My brother and I learned right from wrong, what we could do and what was 'not done'.

We grew up having many aunts, uncles and cousins, friends and neighbours. My parents were both aged 23 when they married, the year the First World War began. Dad must have been called into the army quite soon. I have only ever seen one picture of him in uniform but I believe he served in Dublin. My brother, Ronald Sidney James was born in June 1916 at home. Those were days – and certainly up to the time I was born – when midwifery was not well covered. My parents were not poor but doctors would have to be paid. I don't know if our Dr Scuddamore of Whitehorse Road attended or only the so-called midwife, but Ron was born with a broken collar-bone.

In his early years he developed tuberculosis, but recovered and was sent to convalesce in Weston-Super-Mare. Upon my parents visiting him there he was found to be eating dog biscuits and they took him home. Mother never complained to me about his birth but as I grew up she told the tale to me about her tribulations over my arrival times without number.

There was, however, with me, an added complication. Here I must pause to record what a very strange thing seems to me. Mother often said to me that when she married she was ignorant, she meant of the facts of life. That is hard to understand. Herself a twin, she and Grace had eight siblings, five born after them and two before, and she didn't know what it was all about? Anyway, my parents were told by the doctor after Ron's birth, not to have more children. It was seven years before she was pregnant again, with me, and too frightened to tell the kindly doctor. She often said "They didn't tell us how not to". Their relationship during those seven years almost defies imagination.

So I was on the way. Mother did attend an antenatal clinic and apparently I was turned a couple of times but still presented eventually feet-or bottom-first in July 1923. Dr Scuddamore was not called soon enough. He may not have known Mother was pregnant. My body was delivered, my right arm being pulled out last, thus severing muscles and nerves of my right shoulder (Ron – broken collarbone, me

– damaged arm? Same midwife?) I never needed to ask about this as Mother told it to me throughout my life with friends and neighbours hearing the tale nearly as frequently. Of course it was a horrendous experience for her and she was entitled to such outbursts, full of emotional frustration as she must have been, but I never knew what to answer her. I did ask about the midwife, who was she, etc., and apparently she was 'called before a committee'. My father never joined in nor spoke a word to me about any of it. Certainly there was no family comforting to my knowledge. There, I have told you the details now as I am the only one who knows. If anyone reads this, now you know the truth about it.

In my later life, I can see that there was fear, guilt, stupidity and negligence. What were they doing, trusting to luck? I have enormous anger inside me which has had to be kept under control. Perhaps by writing it here the anger is being given an outlet. My disability is low on the list compared with many, but it is mine and I have had to live with it. It seems a poor time to have been born, medically, as there were many children born with similar disadvantages. But I think of victims of the thalidomide tragedy and other terrible happenings, then mine pales into insignificance. With two good arms I would have been an entirely different person.

My grandmother Goldsmith, upon visiting the new mother and baby, was the first one to say, "What's wrong with her arm?" Nobody else seems to have noticed. The doctor promptly arranged for attention at Great Ormond Street Hospital. Here I must express enormous praise and gratitude to the doctors and staff there for their skill and concern. Mother, of course, (poor Mother) had to take me, a babe in arms, to London frequently thereafter for treatment. Lifting my arm and seeing it fall, the doctor announced *'paralysis*. Mother called it Infantile Paralysis, which was wrong, as that is polio. She didn't care what it was called, it was just a horrible occurrence.

The arm was put up in a splint and remained so for 18 months, in an attempt to repair the damage. It probably helped, but left the arm one inch shorter than the other. I have a very early memory of seeing the glass-panelled roof of a vast area above me and I think this must have been what I saw as Mother carried me, probably at Victoria Station. What a peculiar baby I must have looked with one arm strapped in an L-shape above my head. I try not to apportion blame – things were very different in those days.

I am told I was a screaming baby much of the time and I am not surprised. Surely I knew something was wrong. Babies like to wave arms and legs about; even today my brain, being strongly right-handed, says to me, "use it, use it" but the arm cannot lift itself. The hospital ordered ongoing physiotherapy to make the forearm and hand work well, and I am eternally grateful to Sister Oliver and a Scottish nurse at Croydon General Hospital for their twice-weekly devoted care and attention for many years. From then on I must lift the right hand, usually by its thumb, until the elbow is supported, and now in my older age my body finds any use of it quite wearying.

I do not ask for sympathy, but understanding is helpful.

The First Eight Years

With Mother on a day out.

Number 13 Guildford Road, West Croydon, was a small back-to-back house having a narrow passageway from the front door. To the left was the Front Room containing the piano, arm chairs, a small decorative table and short, bobbled curtain hanging from the mantelpiece above the fireplace. Next the stairway to the two bedrooms, the front one was for my parents and Ron and I shared the back room for a few years. The living room, kitchen and cold larder were at the end of the passage. In the fireplace in the living room stood a range which was black-leaded daily, and a gas cooker with rings for saucepans was in the kitchen. There were two steps down to the kitchen, a style frequently found in terraced houses of that time although I can think of no particular reason for that feature. There was a strip of back garden which was kept tidy with bushes and flowers. The lavatory was outside, built into the wall behind the kitchen. Guildford Road was clean, neat and tidy, and in a respectable but not affluent area. This was a time of world financial difficulties leading to the depression years. If you had a job you held onto it.

There were several children living along the road and we played in our gardens. My particular friend to start school with was Audrey Thomson who lived at No. 63. Audrey started a few months earlier than me but as I was born in late July I just scraped into the same school year. Here I must make a point which can be linked into later thoughts: Audrey's parents were Bob and Lil, both very pleasant, in fact long-lasting friends to my mother, and much loved and respected by Audrey and her elder sister Eileen. They were probably the first people in Guildford Road to have a telephone; it was for Bob's business – he was a horseracing bookie and he worked at home. Lil reassured my mother, whose upbringing had taught her that racing and betting were wrong and you don't associate with such people, that "We are not wicked people, Mrs Goldsmith".

Bob was an enthusiastic crossword solver, a pastime introduced in newspapers about that time. One day I went to call for Audrey and I saw her mother sitting in front of the fire; she obviously had a cold but seemed to be sad about something. Bob bent and kissed Lil's forehead and put a comforting arm around her. I had never seen my father do that to my mother. I remember it so clearly. There was no fuss. Now, of course, I know the tension that existed between my parents, but I find it very sad. In later years such comforting would have greatly benefited our family.

My mother sang around the house, very sweetly and in tune, mostly "Won't you buy my pretty flowers?", but that was as far as her appreciation of music went. My Grandma Goldsmith was a natural musician who could play and sing well. Dad owned a piano, a pretty awful old thing, but he had some of his mother's musical ability and I think he had perfect pitch, as I have. When they were newly married, he tried to teach Mother to read music but she didn't take it seriously and found it a joke. So there ended his efforts. But I have happy memories of coming home from school, Mother and me sitting by the glowing range, having our tea, listening to the orchestras and singers of the day and to the delightful Children's Hour.

The wireless was a new invention; Dad and Ron put together a pack described then as cat's whiskers, erected a pole in the garden for the aerial and Lo! There was magic. I was enthralled even at that young age by Jack Payne and his orchestra, Henry Hall, Victor Sylvester and others. It was the beginning of the days of the glorious singable, harmonious music of Jerome Kern, Cole Porter, George Gershwin and all the lyric writers. Dad and Ron were also busy at early DIY developing photos which were spread open to the sun on the ledge of an open window and gave us sepia prints. In due course we progressed to proper equipment as the market boomed.

Being my senior by seven years, when I started school Ron was already doing well at the piano and showing impressive ability. He had been put to lessons with Miss Irene Burr, a friend of my aunts Doris and Ruby and organist and choir mistress at their church. Irene had the letters LRAM after her name, which I learned meant Licentiate of The Royal Academy of Music. At a very early age I wanted those letters and I got them in due course, a double LRAM about which I will write later.

Ron's lessons with Irene cost three shillings and sixpence for half an hour. I was sent to a Miss Walker who charged one shilling and sixpence for half an hour. Knowing nothing of jealousy, I just accepted that he came first but from then I knew there was a low expectancy of me, not only in music but generally a negative attitude. So often I heard, "She can't do that because of her arm". In fact I had very soon found that I had another arm which could help in the doing of many but not all things. Thus I believe that I became aware that I must be a fighter and find things in life that I certainly could do.

Of course Ron was worth the expensive lessons, but he had two good arms and in years to come I superseded him in musical study and achievement. I got on very well with Miss Walker, she was a fine teacher who acknowledged the musician in me and encouraged me. We worked well together for three years but my being good enough to be a professional solo pianist was unlikely as there were things my arm could not sufficiently cope with, like trills and turns. If I sit high enough I can get the arm to the keyboard and lift it by shoulder muscles.

"Ron could play the piano before he was five years old" Mother told everybody. What they chose not to notice was that at the age of five I was in my first school play and one girl had to sing a little ditty. I went home and played it on the piano with consummate ease, just from hearing it, the piano part as well as the melody. It is still with me. Nobody noticed. Move over, Mozart! I have always had that ability to write down what I hear, in full score if necessary. Music is in my head all day. It is no problem to me, together with sight reading, transposition and improvisation, but I have never studied composition so Mozart is well ahead, you'll be glad to hear.

There are many musicians who can take musical dictation and others who cannot. Mozart remains supreme for his many other attributes and abilities with which he produced such brilliance, innovation, progression, elegance, love and beauty. All praise to him for transcribing what he heard in the Sistine Chapel in Rome – Allegri's Miserere, but there are six verses sung quite slowly. It was a great thing that he did, releasing such a treasure to the musical world. It is fine to have abilities and to use them.

Childhood was filled with pleasures, relations visiting, picnic outings to local beauty and play spots. Shirley Hills in particular, which involved meeting cousins, aunts and uncles and the long walk up Shirley Road past the windmill, family photos taken on the flat space at the top, trees to climb and ball games. Sometimes we met Goldsmith cousins Eileen and Malcolm; they were grandchildren of Uncle James and their parents were Stanley James Haddon Goldsmith and his wife Lena Ellicott.

One particular memory is of Aunt Annie Goldsmith calling for us in her chauffeur-driven Rolls Royce, and together with her daughter Doris and her two children, taking us to the seaside for the day. Aunt Annie was the wife of Jabez James Goldsmith (JJ), brother to my grandfather. James was a man of importance in Croydon, indeed a JP, and they lived at 99 Uplands Road, Sutton, in a detached house which they called 'Wallbourne' because Annie had been a Miss Wall from Bourne in Lincolnshire.

They employed a maid in their house which greatly impressed Ron and me. I imagine that was normal home life for Annie but I think the chauffeur was to drive James around town in an appropriate manner. He was also secretary at West Croydon Baptist Church as I grew up and he made the weekly announcements.

There were often train trips to south coast resorts, Brighton was nearest, Eastbourne, Bognor Regis, Portsmouth, Southsea, Hastings and others. We had family at Portsmouth; Dad's brother Horace, Auntie Gladys and my cousin May lived there. May was born in Portsmouth but we visited their home at Southsea frequently. May, sadly no longer with us, was a good musician and we have often played piano duets. She and I were of similar age and tastes and both valued our long and enduring relationship.

Sometimes our trips were further afield; once at Margate when I was about three years old they managed to lose me and had to send out a search party. Another time

Mother and Dad fancied a visit to Epsom races to watch the Derby and they lost me again. I remember being carried yelling, high in a policeman's arms. Later, on holiday at Hastings, Ron put his hand on my head and held me under the water. I was frightened but survived. Seems like a message there for me.

Aunt Ethel Goldsmith, Dad's sister, was a weekly visitor at Guildford Road. She came for her tea after work and I was taught to clean and re-set the table after I had eaten, for her or whoever would follow me. A good lesson in consideration for others (even if it was only my brother). So I was expected to speak and behave properly. Dad used to bring home packets of twisted paper which, when placed in a saucer of water would magically open and become beautiful flowers. They were certainly Japanese.

Auntie Ethel Goldsmith

Always I was bought good Christmas presents. One year it was a marvellous book which opened showing various 3D stage settings and pull-out characters which I could place as in a theatre. Another year a large beautiful china doll which I named Sylvia. Dad always liked a table to be nicely laid and I still follow that idea.

Visits from Aunties Ruth and Ruby were especially delightful and took me on their knees for cuddles. They always admired anything I had done and they overflowed with love.

I enjoyed both schools I attended. After my fifth birthday my first was Holy Trinity School at Selhurst. It was officially attached to Holy Trinity Church next door to it but I don't remember ever going into the church. The only connection was with one of the teachers who made us bow our heads whenever we said or sang 'Jesus'. Musically we were much blessed; we had three teachers who could play the piano to our singing and I was impressed.

Our first year infants' teacher was Miss Chambers and we thought she had a very rude name. Miss Pearce next and she taught us to read and write. She read Alice in Wonderland to us in short sessions. End of term and rise to the next year class prevented her from telling us how Alice got out of the rabbit hole and it puzzled me for a long time. Through the years we had Miss Ferris who made the classroom her school home and would not move to another. There was an old-fashioned cylindrical iron stove with a tall smoke pipe. She stoked it in winter and kept us all warm.

With her we grew runner beans on blotting paper, kept tadpoles, acted plays, learned some lessons and she started us on watercolour painting. The following year was with Mrs Crispin who soon retired. Miss Nimmo was tall, very pleasant and one of our pianists. She introduced us to A.A. Milne's Christopher Robin which was newly published in song form. I wondered why Christopher Robin had needles at the foot of his bed. Think about it. Then a Miss Pierce, chiefly noticed for being a bit overcome in the two-minutes' silence one 11th November.

In the top 10-11year-olds class we had a wonderful and remarkable teacher whom I shall never forget. She was a widow, Mrs MacFarland, quite short in stature, Scottish, challenging, and it was her job to get us through the examination which lay in the immediate future – the 11 Plus, our passport to secondary education. Macky, as we called her, always took time to explain things, such as how little time it takes to erase or cross out a wrong letter or word and replace it with the correct one. Nobody can read alterations. Also how few seconds it takes to write out something mathematical, then you understand it. Many more things we learned from her. She was most kind to me in a special way. For regular physiotherapy I had to visit hospital twice each week. I must have come out of school and gone by tram. The forearm and hand were skilfully exercised with loving care for many years but, of course, this meant loss of vital school work. I remember Mrs Mac asking me to bring olive oil so that she could massage my arm, which she did in her own time.

In warm summer weather we played out in the playground and sometimes had lessons outside. One day all of us were called out as a small plane flew overhead and we waved to Amy Johnson.

When I was eight years old we moved house from Guildford Road to Lodge Road, the first of 22 moves in my life which would come about, and here in my story enters a woman named Miss Llewellyn.

A New House

There was no need for a change of school so I continued at Holy Trinity, belonging to the same community. My daily walks to and from school were doubled so that for five days a week I walked a mile each way four times. School hours were 9 a.m. to midday, two hours lunch break then 2 p.m. till 4 p.m. I didn't mind the walks, except for one small area through which I had to pass. A local foundry run by Gillett & Johnson, well known in bell-making circles, created work there. Whether, with poor wages, that helped develop a slum area I don't know, but I had to pass Wilford Road and a few others which were very run down and frightening because of drunken behaviour.

Holy Trinity Church and school

Auntie Ruby ran a mission hall there and sought to bring light and joy into the lives of these men and women. Sometimes Mother and I joined them in coach parties to seaside places. One trip was to Southend-on-Sea and one to Penshurst Place, we had a beautiful and memorable day there. I have often wanted to go there again. Hopefully these slums have since been cleared.

Left behind now were The Thomson family, The Baxters at No. 15 who had non-identical twins, Marjorie and Lily, and The Russells at No. 11. Mother and Mrs Russell used to talk together over the fence, very properly, no 'common' talk. From indoors we heard mostly, "Yes, Mrs Russell" and "No, Mrs Russell" from Mother. This very kind lady knitted for me a pretty pink silk dress when I was about three years old and later I earned pennies from her for running errands to the shops.

Also I was glad my father no longer would nearly rub me out with his fierce hair-drying. In the new house we would have a proper bathroom and I was growing up.

I began to hear the name Miss Llewellyn spoken and she sometimes came to us for Sunday tea, together with some Sunday School teachers. Miss Llewellyn seemed to me young, fair-haired, pink complexioned and like a soft cushion.

Now behind me were my first three school years. Ron had been at school locally before I was born and by the time I was eight he had gained a scholarship to John Ruskin Grammar School. To me he seemed very grown up and our lives were largely separate. I still have a vivid memory of him in a Scouts' annual pantomime, performed at Stanley Halls, South Norwood. In the story of Robin Hood, Ron was Maid Marian and he sang, dressed (rather unwillingly) in a long yellow robe, at the front of the stage, "Just a Song at Twilight". I was very proud of him. His voice was still soprano.

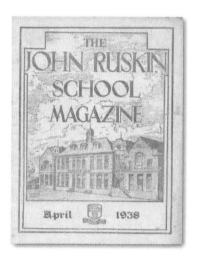

The Lodge Road house was modern with two reception rooms, kitchen, bathroom, etc., two good bedrooms and a small one for me, rear garden and a long front garden. We understood Miss Llewellyn found it for us, at a rental twice that of the previous house. It suited us very nicely and we were only a few doors away from Dad's cousin Stanley with Auntie Lena, Eileen and Malcolm, my Goldsmith cousins. They also had the use of the chauffeur which was good sometimes for our party-going.

To explain Miss Llewellyn I must go into family church-going. Up to that time I think I had only gone to West Croydon Baptist with Mother, Grandma and aunts, but now I became aware that my father attended somewhere else. He was indeed using his musical abilities as organist and choirmaster at a mission hall called Joynson Memorial Hall, an offshoot of WC Baptist. Well, good for him; that gave him much satisfaction, but my parents going to different places of worship was to cause great upset in our lives. I became pulled between the two of them. Apart from having been married there, I never knew my father go to the big church. He was firmly dug in and relied upon at The Hall, some evenings as well as Sundays. It seems that besides the music, a certain young lady, one of the workers at The Hall, also had some pull in that direction. I once asked him what was Miss Llewellyn's first name. He did tell me, it was Welsh but I cannot remember it.

Dad was also treasurer to the mission and of necessity had to linger in the back vestries to count the takings, didn't he? While I waited outside. I hated that mission place. It was claustrophobic and whilst the regular folk were kind and welcoming to me, in my mind it was not where I wanted to be. Sometimes I sang the alto part with his choir because I could read the music and understood the harmonies.

One Sunday evening I had been put to bed in my little room; Ron was out somewhere with his teenage companions, Dad had gone to The Hall. I could hear Mother getting ready to go to church but I didn't want to be left alone in the house. Determined to go, she was looking in drawers for her attendance ticket for the monthly communion service. It was not that my parents were deeply religious but they were churchgoers and that was their way of life. If Mother missed a certain number of attendances at communion she could be denied church membership, which would have been a disgrace to her. Dad never in all his life spoke a religious word to me nor in my hearing, neither did Mother. Is it any wonder I bit my nails? She never found the ticket that night. No, I had nothing to do with it.

Mother's lack of musical understanding often made the situation hilarious. She was infrequently persuaded to go to The Hall when Dad's choir gave a performance, which he led from the harmonium. On sitting through the Amen chorus (not the whole work, I assure you!) of Handel's Messiah, her quite reasonable comment was "Why do they keep singing Amen? They've sung it once".

More devastating remarks from Mother throughout the years:-

Ron had bought an Erard piano (at a later house) and invited a violinist friend of his to come so that they could make music together. Mother's comment, in front of the visitor, was "Of course, the violin is nothing without the piano, is it?"

At age 17 years I began to take singing lessons and was asked to perform to visiting company. I played and sang a song, and Mother said apologetically "She has to do that with her mouth, her teacher tells her to".

Many years later, when I was driving her from Berkhamsted through London to her home in Croydon, a journey I had done many times, she said "Fancy YOU finding your way through here!" Thank you, Mother, I can read and write too.

We enjoyed our new home where we could spread ourselves. Mother could easily walk the shorter distance for her daily visit to St James's Road, Dad could cycle to work and to The Hall past the long cemetery wall in Pawson's Road, Ron could cycle to John Ruskin School and I carried on walking. When I reached the old home ground I could meet my usual friends. The rear garden was for sitting in and playing and the front garden stretched quite a long way.

Gardening became an enthusiasm with many annuals and bushes. Cosmos were very popular, together with Antirrhinums, Lobelia and Californian Poppies. By the front gate were two trees, one of which was a Laburnum. It was from here that Grandfather Clutterbuck's sister, Little Auntie Flo, took me to Belvedere in Kent during one summer holiday where I met my step-great-grandmother and her daughter Aunt Lily. The old lady was in the garden picking runner beans when we arrived. She seemed to have no teeth; I hope I didn't stare too rudely.

At home, there was another of Grandfather's sisters living nearby at No. 7 Farquharson Road. This was his youngest sister Amy Elizabeth and she lived with a Miss Carter. We never knew that lady's name. Amy was rather small but a very smart, cultured and lively lady and these two friends held card evenings, very happy times which became boisterous over Whist, Snap, Rummy, Pit and a game called Thank You, and others. Afterwards they served sandwich suppers. After Miss Carter had died, Aunt Amy spent some of her last months at my parents' home and she left my mother £100 for taking care of her. She was a lovely lady, and when she died in 1963 she endowed a room in her name at Burrell Mead in West Wickham, Kent.

It is time I mentioned the Guildford, Surrey, connection where Auntie Grace, Mother's twin, was living with her husband Herbert Jones and his three children, Richard (Dick), Ronald – almost the same age as my brother – and Muriel who was two years my senior. The twins could never be far away from each other. Croydon and Guildford are about thirty miles apart but this distance was easily covered by train and/or No. 408 green double-decker bus to and from West Croydon.

Uncle Bert was manager of a motor parts business in Denzil Road and he often travelled from there to report to his boss, a Mr Moore who lived in Croydon. He came to our house for a meal before leaving for home and I frequently went with him on the train back to Guildford, creeping into bed beside Cousin Muriel. This was home from home; I was always accepted there by all the family and thus escaped some of the tension in my own home. I am told that on a very early visit I announced that I was "goin' home in a minit", but far from that, I would have stayed there for ever given the chance.

Dick opened a cycle shop when he left school and married Dorothy in due course. The two Rons were good friends and we all got on well together. Christmases there were memorable as full family gatherings. The weather then always seemed to fit the seasons. The Jones family lived in Agraria Road, off the Farnham Road at the foot of the Hog's Back, a beautiful spot in beautiful Surrey.

Dick's Bicycle Shop

Muriel and I walked many miles all around, often with Auntie's Airedale dog. One favourite way was along Farnham Road until we reached the turn off for Compton, through that village, out into the Portsmouth Road and back into Guildford, finally up the hill again to home. What a distance! Compton was an enchanting village where we visited the G.F. Watts Art Gallery and the wonderful old church, although I only discovered the latter in later years.

Here's a strange point. The twins had been brought up to avoid alcohol, as their church taught them. My father "never touched a drop" and Uncle Bert seemed of the same opinion. My Grandfather Goldsmith liked his beer but we never spent Christmas with Dad's folk. I clearly remember, though, that the grownups at our Christmases had a bottle or two of Port each Yuletide, also that Mother collected dandelion flowers from the fields in season and made wine from them. At my wedding and on my twenty-first birthday there were only soft drinks. What a muddle.

Whilst we lived at Lodge Road, I went to play on Saturday mornings with my cousin Hilda, Uncle Will's daughter, at their London Road home. Later when David was a baby we proudly wheeled him out for a few hours in our leisure time. This was a very normal thing to do, part of our culture, that responsible young people - or grandmas – could keep the babies or toddlers happily occupied this way for a few hours. Sadly, Hilda is no longer with us but I still hear annually from David.

In previous pages perhaps I have presented myself as a good little girl. Certainly I was not rebellious at home, it would have done me no good. With my brother while he was still at junior school, I laughed at the silly jokes schoolboys bring home and learnt rude rhymes. We even enjoyed Children's Hour together sometimes. I began to misbehave at Sunday School (W. Croydon Baptist, of course) and entertained our group during the stories, until a family friend whispered in my ear "I'll have to have a word with your father". That stopped me although I can't imagine that anything would have happened.

Ron had done well at his Grammar school, excelled at Art and French language, which news was sent around the family, especially about French. My school days were working up to the 11 Plus examination and our headmistress, Miss Tozer, against the rules I believe, took a few of us from the top class into coaching sessions. Miss Tozer was not an approachable person and could make scathing remarks. In fact she was a good introduction to my next headmistress at my new school who seemed even more distant, although I did grow to respect her. We moved house again and I changed from one school to another.

Changes

With my brother, Ronald – my dress was knitted by Mrs Russell.

My father was very good at his office job; he had a tidy mind, neat handwriting and a good knowledge of the local area. At school he had been good at English, arithmetic and map drawing and he had always guided me well in the social business of writing thank you and sympathy letters, also job applications. Both Mother and

Dad wanted Ron and me to speak well and be good citizens.

We were happy enough in our way of life apart from the underlying split over church-going. It was now 1934 and the government's great house-building project was rapidly spreading, bringing us ribbon development. Long streets came into being where once were fields, with fewer terraces and more detached and semi-detached properties. Maybe Dad was promoted and his salary increased as he began seeking a house in the Shirley Hills area. This time he intended to buy instead of renting. We settled in due course in Ridgemount Avenue, Shirley, Croydon, just off Wickham Road which led to West Wickham, Kent. Great excitement. This was a lovely house on a new estate, with a good front garden and a long one to the rear, pretty tiled fireplaces and an adjoining garage, it cost the princely sum of £900. My brother soon found an office job with the building company. He was 18 years old and quickly learned the smoking habit, among other things, from his new colleagues.

19 Ridgemount Avenue, Shirley – slightly altered from new.

Dad and Mother worked very hard creating new gardens, building a terrace and a rockery with steps down, laying lawns and decorative paths. Good stone was available from the firm, no doubt at a staff discount. A car was bought, a handsome Fiat, and we acquired a telephone. I was installed at Lady Edridge School at South Norwood and cycled there and back each day. Never being unduly worried about exams, or maybe I didn't try hard enough in the 11 Plus, Grammar school evaded me. I had, though, lost a lot of valuable schooling whilst at Holy Trinity.

My first school friend, Audrey Thomson, had proceeded to Selhurst Grammar School. I went to my new school and enjoyed it enormously. My family hadn't expected great things from me anyway. My only disappointment was that Audrey's school had a pleasant, approachable headmistress but my new one was not promising in that direction. Miss Ethel Mayhew was a fine educationalist and strict disciplinarian, with great plans for her girls and the high standing of her school, but she was very severe.

If Mother had been hoping that when the new move was accomplished Dad would sever his links with The Hall and Miss Llewellyn, she must have been bitterly disappointed. Dad was away several weekday evenings and every Sunday, leaving Mother to spend long hours alone or with just me. I often heard her pleading with him to spend more time at home but he was committed. I could understand both sides of the situation but didn't know what could be done about it and found it distressing. Maybe there was no harm happening but Mother was entitled to some companionship.

The Thomson family had also moved house to a new one on South Norwood Hill. I was visiting Audrey one evening; as I was about to leave we heard the 9 o'clock news radio announcer say, "The Crystal Palace is on fire!"

Indeed it was, and we ran into the garden and saw the glowing sky. As the crow flies the palace was quite close. It seems I was out late that night. Mother was, sadly, in Croydon hospital at the time, having a hysterectomy. Two buses took me home to Shirley and there, from our bedroom windows we watched this tremendous fire.

Other memorable events of that year, 1936, were the death of King George V, the accession of Edward VIII and his subsequent abdication and George VI becoming the new monarch. New subjects to learn at school were exciting to me; English, geography, history, biology, mathematics, algebra, geometry, science etc. Best of all were French and music. Again we had some musical teachers; the best of these, Miss Williams, played records of classical music to us and formed a school choir in which I could lead in the harmony line, with some others. Miss Capel, our maths teacher also taught us country dancing, which I loved and could mostly manage the arm movements. French was my highlight though; I fell into it as if it were my own language. Our mistress was a French woman, Miss Mallet, and her teaching was basic and helpful. Science I liked and in spite of doing a spell of entertaining the class, for which I narrowly avoided being sent to the headmistress, I was top of the class.

In retrospect the language and general teaching we had in those days seems to have been so logical and memorable. Teachers were respected and must have had good wages as many were able to go abroad for holidays. Our playground was the adjacent local Recreation Ground. In wet weather we stayed indoors and did ballroom dancing in lunch-hours, with pupils who were able playing the piano. I was sometimes one of them. I still love dancing but partners I have found in my life have either been married or had two left feet.

I recall myself sitting on the terrace at home doing my French homework, working towards a Royal Society of Arts examination. The link with music here is now obvious: they are both languages and they make sense to me. I sat the exam and came top, not only of my form entrants but those a year ahead of me. This was announced at assembly and I was thrilled. However, nobody at home thought anything of it, nor of my science success. The news did not go around the family and I don't recall any word of praise from my parents. I don't think they knew what it meant. The school, however, had plans for a trip to Paris on which I was expected to go but life had other plans for me. Soon I would have to leave school and be plunged into the world of work. We moved to Guildford. Miss Mayhew wrote me a reference saying:-

"Freda Goldsmith was a pupil of this school from September 1934 to April 1938. The removal of her parents to Guildford was the cause of her leaving. We found her a most satisfactory pupil and were sorry to lose her. Her work in general had reached a good standard and her English was well above the average for her age. I can well recommend her for I am confident she will prove an efficient and trustworthy worker.
Ethel M Mayhew (Miss) Headmistress.

A good, generous report. I had not known she was aware of me but the fault would have been mine as a naïve teenager.

I have jumped ahead, perhaps because it is painful to put on paper what happened in 1938, but I will do so because it is a true record. I must have been on school holiday for I had spent the day with my father in his car as he visited his firm's customers. Now a travelling representative, he would advise people on the running of their new IDEAL water-heating boilers and collect money from those who were paying their bills through him. As we reached home, before getting out of the car he said to me "You and I are good pals, aren't we?" as if needing assurance. I thought it was a bit strange. Mother and Dad and I went to a concert that evening at the North End Halls, a venue in the Kennards building, a big department store in Croydon. The entertainers included a young Terence Alexander and the star of the show, Arthur Askey. Dad seemed quiet, puffing away at his pipe whilst everyone else was laughing. At home I heard them both come to bed, then suddenly all hell broke loose. Ron and I were called to join them downstairs. Apparently an unpaid bill at the newsagent's, then a phone call from Dad's office had alerted Mother to the fact that they had not seen my father for a week or so. Was he at home unwell? Would he be coming to work tomorrow?

Mother was hysterical, justifiably, as the words came from him – "There's money missing from the firm" and he had been suspended. So where had he been driving me all that day and where had he gone every day if not to the office? Then we heard "I was going to pay it back". What with?

It was impossible to take in all that it meant that night. Ron and I felt sympathy for him because it was not the kind of thing he normally would do, and especially as Mother's reaction was frightening and not helpful. Of course, to her it was the end of everything. They both were called to the office and explanations and fears had to surface. But he lost his job, we lost the house, the car and whatever we had planned for the future. The firm, and others, would have helped him had he asked. All the families had to know. He still had connection with the folk at the mission hall where he was also treasurer, but we will not go down that road.

Eventually we retired to bed in silent distress, not knowing what to make of this situation. What clearly stands out to me now is that there were no comforting arms for each other, neither that night nor at any time. We knew not how to show love or comfort each other and there was great emotional deprivation. I never heard the word 'sorry' from anyone. Ron was safely earning his own living but I was pulled out of my school from which I would have had a chance to follow other schoolmates to Cambridge. Well, that's what life does and it's no good complaining. After some weeks a job had been found for my father in Guildford (probably with help from the Joneses) and the move to Guildford took place.

Guildford!! – perhaps life could be pleasant again.

Heading for the War Years

The Jones family at Newlands Corner c1924

Back: L-R Richard (Dick) Uncle Bert, Uncle Tom

Front: Dorothy, Ronald, Auntie Grace and Muriel

Uncle Bert had a billiards table in his front room and the family men had enjoyed many hours of play over the years. They named our joint families Smithies, Jones & Co. They would have loved to watch today's snooker players and footballers on television. A quiet man generally, Uncle Bert was generous, kindly and took life at his own pace but diligently. Billiards got them away from the chattering twins and the children - Muriel and me.

In the fairly early days of radio, an exciting moment was when connecting leads and speakers allowed the radio to be heard from one room to another. Muriel and I slept in the bedroom above the living room and on Christmas Eve we could hear decorations being hung downstairs. The tree was in the front room and only revealed on Christmas Day. Aunt Grace would make a Bran Tub and we really knew what family Christmas meant. The table received a protective, padded layer and on top were laid the festive meals, with about a dozen family members seated around.

Auntie Grace - my mother's twin

My father's misdeeds had been accepted as regrettable but after the shock he needed to be helped back to stability. I cannot remember whether both Rons were married by 1938. My brother did not move with us to our new address at 'Ebury', Bray Road, Guildford, parallel to the Joneses' home in Agraria Road, but the two of them often seemed to be around.

The school leaving age then must have been fourteen years as I was now considered to be ready for work. Perhaps I went to an employment exchange and was sent after an office job. What could I do? I didn't know but was offered 10/- per week to start filing papers. This was at the large firm of DENNIS, makers of buses, fire vehicles, engines, etc. I said no to their 10/- and, unbelievably now, they agreed on 12/6d. Small fish in a large pond.

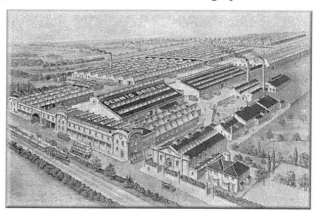

After a few months, cousin Ron found me a better place with the firm he worked for called Angel, Son and Gray, well-known ironmongers, builders, plumbers. I can't get away from ironmongers. Here I had to work the telephone switchboard, answer all calls and generally assist in the office. I learned a lot about life there that was new to me. Soon I took evening tuition in Pitman's shorthand, Ron Jones kindly lent me his typewriter and I taught myself to touch type.

Farnham Road runs from Guildford railway station to the top of the Hog's Back hill, which is on the left-hand side, and on through to Farnham. To the right-hand side, beyond Agraria and Bray roads and all the houses in between, is Stag Hill, upon which stands Guildford cathedral. While we were living there, concrete piles were being driven into the hill in preparation for the foundations of the new building. I have never been inside the cathedral but certainly paid for a brick or two. There was controversy at the time as there already was a church at the top of the town claiming to be the existing cathedral; apparently those who wanted a new one were the winners.

All through the 1930s there was no escaping the appalling political situation; the burning down of the Crystal Palace seemed, with no other reason for it being given, quite likely to have been deliberate government action. It would have been a clear landmark. By September 1939 Chamberlain had indeed declared war on Germany and the terrible years had begun. And they were terrible. Those who say they enjoyed the war no doubt enjoyed the purposefulness of combined effort. It is difficult to write about wartime and our experiences because it all sounds tedious, unreal, ghastly and almost unbelievable. Apart from the tragedies, of which there were so many, what happened for the next five years was a great re-shuffling of our lives, thoughts, desires and directions. Young people from 18 years old were called to the forces or to war work and we had no choice of what we wanted to do with our futures. Some survived, many did not, but to dwell on the down side does no good. We can but remember and hopefully learn.

With the now present and real fear of air attack, throughout the first year, many children in vulnerable areas were sent by their parents, on government advice and insistence, to less dangerous places. Guildford took in many such evacuees and two sisters of about ten and six years were sent to our home. They stayed for a few months but my mother was not the best person to be looking after somebody else's children. She would never have harmed them but their mother came to take them home after a short time as they missed their own home. This was not uncommon; not all evacuees found satisfactory second homes and as the war did not immediately become serious, many parents wanted their children back with them. I hope our two survived without trouble.

Towards D-Day, 6th June 1944, and throughout earlier years when troops were being moved towards the south of England and businesses were moving northwards to make room for them, Aunt Grace and family had three soldiers billeted on them, also two charming and important-seeming women. What an upheaval, but how exciting.

I loved my surroundings; the sight of the Hog's Back hill from the very top of the town, the cobbled High Street, the Pilgrim's Way through the top of the Hog's Back towards St Mary's Chapel, the surrounding villages of Bramley, Shere with its Silent Pool, Abinger Hammer with the chiming clock and watercress beds, Merrow

Downs, Compton and the field nearby where primroses grew abundantly. We often gathered bunches of these, until one day a gamekeeper appeared with his gun, telling us we were trespassing on private property. We withdrew.

Another nearby village was Chilworth where cousin Ron Jones became leader of a religious crusading-mission group, holding meetings in the village hall. As I could play the piano it seemed inevitable that I went along with this activity but in time I knew it all was not for me, nor was I dedicated enough to be of any greater use. Ron was set upon the path of his convictions. A young lady named Irene Lambley who, with her mother, ran the local greengrocer's shop, delivered weekly provisions to us all. She was a staunch Salvation Army girl and in due course Ron and Rene married.

But there was a war on, re-arranging everybody.

Dick and Dorothy celebrate their Diamond Wedding

Ron Jones and Freda to the left.

Leslie and Stephen – Muriel's sons

Back to Croydon

Freda back from Australia - 1960

Dates escape me but I know that Father, Mother and I were living in Croydon again by mid-1940, in time to see the beginning of the Battle of Britain; in fact, from our bedroom windows we again could watch a spectacular event. This may have been the first air battle, over Croydon Airport, not far away. We could see planes dipping and diving and persons descending in parachutes. It was very frightening and a terrifying confirmation that worse was likely to come.

Dad's job at Guildford had folded, not through any fault of his, and he was now working at Wallington, between Croydon and Sutton. As he had spare evenings (no more connection at The Hall so far as I knew) he became a Home Guard. Stationed very close to home, there was a lot for these guards to do during air raids. We suffered from bombs, V1s and V2s known as Doodle Bugs, landmines and unexploded bombs, night after night and often in the daytime. We had to leave our home for a few days because of the latter. I managed to persuade a policeman to let me go back in to feed and comfort our cat.

On 24th May 1941 a dear uncle of mine, Father's brother Horace was killed on active Royal Naval Reserve service, to the great distress of his wife Auntie Gladys and my cousin May. We lost some close friends and acquaintances but were lucky to suffer so little.

My father suggested I might apply for a job he had seen advertised. He thought it might suit me because it was a religious organisation and I was then continuing to attend church as I had been brought up to do. I found myself attached to The Lord's Day Observance Society as a shorthand typist. No questions were asked as to what thoughts I had on the subject of Sunday. I guess I just fitted. I had no thoughts, actually.

My time with the LDOS was quite a revelation. The office staff were female and great to work and be with. We did the menial work like opening envelopes, taking down other people's thoughts, typing letters, taking money to the bank, etc., whilst various men who thought they were important strutted about attending meetings and condemning those who saw life differently. As a charity each day the LDOS received money in the post in response to appeals; many small amounts of 2/- or 2/6d arrived from pensioners.

With the heavy bombing of London, journeys to and from work became very difficult. Many times I had to walk a long part of my way to work – then in Red Lion Square at the Theobalds Road end of Kingsway – in central London as the trams I boarded from home could not get through the bomb-debris-littered streets of Brixton. One day on arriving we saw our offices were completely razed to the ground, as was much of Red Lion Square. People were being stretchered out of collapsed buildings, dead or alive. Within a short time we were re-housed in Finchley Road, NW London, nearly opposite the underground station.

I remember my female colleagues with affection though, and learned valuable life-lessons there. One of the elderly gentlemen bosses, Mr Bolton, took kindly to me, partly because he was a church organist and so was I then, well I was a deputy locally and we could talk music together. One summer's day he took me to tea at the Savoy Hotel in Piccadilly and on to see the beautiful massed roses at Queen Mary's Gardens in Regent's Park. I don't remember how we got time off but he was the boss.

My time with the society ended in 1941 with my call-up to serve my country. There was a written intelligence test which I was told I had passed impressively, but on seeing my passive right arm hanging by my side the doctor had no choice but to fail me. I couldn't salute any officers. I wonder where life would have taken me had that door not shut? Papers soon arrived directing me to work for

Mullard Radio Valve Company at Mitcham, which I learned was joined to the now enormous Philips organisation. My work was only typing and I can't remember what I typed. I cycled to and from Mitcham each day and for the rest of the wartime my life was with that company, moving eventually to their offices in Century House, St Giles Circus, junction of Shaftesbury Avenue and Oxford Street, London.

It was at Mitcham with Mullards that Clifford and I met; he was there, as I was, to do war work. We were both now working in a scientific department on what was called The Island, a stretch of land separated from the main works by the River Wandle. It was quite pleasant there and occasionally I saw a kingfisher diving into the river. I assumed Cliff was there because he was a graduate in Physics and was considered brainy enough to be useful in the work being done in the department. I never really asked. It was many years later that I discovered he had indeed been a conscientious objector and this is a most peculiar fact when I remember that his subsequent employments were with deHavilland, EMI and others, all working enthusiastically on missiles. For example, at deHavilland's he worked on Blue Streak in deadly secrecy.

Clifford in 1958

There is a story to tell here which, in retrospect, has fired my anger against religion and the kind of idiot that my upbringing had made me at that time. I was not worldly-wise like most of my colleagues and must have been fair game for a lark. We were all at Century House by now. One day my boss poked his head round my office door and offered to take me out for a meal one evening. He said his wife was away. Being green as I was, I thought how nice of him. Well, of course, he lost his bet to get me into bed. Years later I realised that's what it was. I am very slow on the uptake.

My department was the first to move to Century House and I noticed that Clifford soon managed to follow. We got along well with each other and on 8th December 1944 we became engaged to be married. I guess we spent the following eight months getting to know our respective friends and relations.

The war was coming to its conclusion, still with ghastly battles and raids occurring but in May of 1945 Germany surrendered, Japan doing so in August. Now free of our wartime occupations, Clifford and I married in August 1945 and set off for our planned honeymoon in Looe, Cornwall, the first time either of us had travelled that far.

Food and clothes rationing were still in force but I managed to have a white wedding with my cousin Muriel as bridesmaid. There was always someone around who knew where goods could be obtained. In my case it was Audrey Thomson's sister Eileen who knew someone in Maida Vale. We followed the trail and had a going-away suit made for me. We had a lovely wedding day.

Cliff owned a car, a Hillman. Petrol rationing, a wartime restriction, was still in operation and during the war his car had been loaned to a colleague who received an allocation. The car was returned and off we went, sublimely ignorant of what troubles to expect. Along the A30 route near Salisbury it developed two punctures and the dreaded Big End trouble, so we had to limp into a garage and spend the night in a Bed and Breakfast, going on to Cornwall next day by train.

We collected it by reverse method on our return, calling in to Aunt Grace for the following night at Guildford. Next morning whilst walking on the Hog's Back hill, Cliff managed to lose his wallet. Not expecting a good result, we asked at the police station and found somebody had very kindly handed it in. Quite an eventful honeymoon.

Our Wedding Day – August 1945

Moving On

Our home for the first few months was a small flat and then we spent a short time at my parents' home. I took a job as a cashier at a local butcher's shop. Clifford was still employed by Mullard/Philips but had been moved to Salfords, near Redhill, so we needed to be nearer that area. His sister Noreen and her husband George Ling were about to sell their house at Woodmansterne, near Banstead, Surrey, and they offered it to us to buy. So that's what we did and Derek was born there in August 1947.

He was a gorgeous baby weighing 9.5 pounds, but he and I spent the first three weeks of his life in Redhill Hospital for my recovery. When I wheeled him out at home a neighbour said, "Oh, he is beautiful" and meant it. I was so proud of him.

Three-and-a-half years later Derek went to stay with my Mum and Dad and I went to Redhill Hospital again where our second son, Graham Edward, was born by caesarean section in April 1951. By this time we had sold the Woodmansterne house and bought another, this time in Earlswood which was even nearer to Cliff's work. Graham

Edward was beautiful too. I loved him and fed him for five days but due to a Rhesus blood condition this little one died. We discovered from the surgeon that there had been a mistake which contributed to his death. At birth the baby's blood was tested but it was believed that the result of that was mixed up with the test of another baby, so my baby missed out on the correct immediate treatment he should have had. Why did we not follow this up this disaster? Today we certainly would have sued the hospital. In a state of deep shock we went home without our baby.

I recall that whilst we were engaged, one day at Streatham I was booked to sing a song of Shakespeare's words at a concert there. Clifford mocked my efforts to sing 'a stupid song' but I soon learned that his rendering of *'I'm 'enery the eighth, I am',* crude words to Greig's Peer Gynt Suite and *'Ave Maria'* sung in falsetto voice were about the limit of his reach of appreciation of music. But we were deeply in love and great companions and were to travel together through life for many years, as you do.

Having started married life with three house moves in two years; that was just the beginning. After Earlswood, by 1953 we were in Aylesbury on Tring Road and Cliff worked for Air Trainers Ltd on early computer development creating simulators to be used for air pilots to train on the ground, and other uses. It was a very pleasant town to live in and it was there that our lovely, lively five-year-old son started school just along the road.

We discovered that we were living next-door-but-one to neighbours who have remained lifelong friends. Stanley Richardson and Clifford recognised each other as having been fellow students at Imperial College, London. Both Stanley and Clifford returned to Imperial College in later years to study and work. With Stanley's wife, Lorna and their three children we shared good times. Derek, and Mary their eldest, started school together at Tring Road Primary. A memorable teacher there was Miss Coldham and the children had a happy start with her. We could see them in their playground from our gardens. Mary's sister Sheila and brother Clive also attended that school.

Stanley and Lorna Richardson remained dear friends

Clifford's parents arrived at our home in January 1954 answering a call for help as I had been taken to Stoke Mandeville Hospital, Wendover, heavily pregnant and stricken with what might have been polio or meningitis, nobody seemed to know. I was very ill, so ill that I have very little memory of my time there, except that I do recall a doctor who came, probably daily, to ask if the baby was moving and listen for its heartbeat. I became aware that he was anxious but he said the baby was probably sleeping. Either I was doped or stupid, but it did not occur to me that had the baby been asleep there still should have been a heartbeat.

Eventually I was taken to the Royal Bucks Hospital, Aylesbury, where I was given a lumbar puncture. Our third baby was induced and still-born in February. I remember such a kind nurse attending me there. In the general rush of days in the maternity ward there was little time to spare for one unlucky patient but this nurse literally gave me her shoulder to cry on and smuggled me tablets which would dry up the milk. Her own mother who was in her eighties was currently recovering from a mastectomy and was joking about wearing 'falsies'.

I write down all these happenings because few people except close friends seem to have known what happened and peculiar stories went round the family. Confusion arose due to the fact that not much was known medically about the Rhesus Negative blood condition at that time. Apparently the blood groups of the parents need to mix satisfactorily to produce healthy babies; should one parent have Rh Negative blood, the first baby will probably be healthy but antibodies will build up in the mother's blood and these work against successive pregnancies.

Modern methods can cope successfully with this jaundice condition by exchanging the baby's blood before it is born. It is heartrending to lose a child whatever the circumstances and I find it painful still. Derek was thus sadly deprived of a brother and sister and Cliff of a larger family.

The illness which knocked me down so completely struck a weak point and left me with further damage to my right arm. It was now less use than before. After much physiotherapy (again) and encouragement from Clifford I could at least get it to the piano keyboard if I sat high enough. Moves to and from Aylesbury were just two of my 22 house moves.

After two years we were on the move again, to Upminster in Essex. Only one of these early moves was because I was unhappy but it had become obvious that after the first day at every new place of work Cliff wanted to move on. Of course we made friends and kept in touch with some of them. At Tring Road we were in Air Trainers' property and thus rented but we bought a newly-built detached house in Upminster, Essex. We must have covered ourselves financially through these transactions but never became affluent.

Derek had to start at a new school and we were concerned that he would have to remain an only child. Cliff was keen for him to have a public school education. We knew he was worth the very best possible. It was a hard thing to do but we carefully sought a good place and settled our lovely boy at Widford Lodge, Chelmsford, not far away from our home.

Derek at Widford Lodge

To find the necessary funds I went back to work, so Upminster being within easy reach of the City I found part-time office employment – temping, right at the hub of London's financial district. I was once at Gracechurch Street with a shipping company, another time with Lloyd's of London. This was in the old building and we employees were sometimes taken round to see its historic objects. We saw the Nelson Room with the table set as it would have been in his time and where the port decanter was believed to first have been passed to the left, also the Lutine Bell which was rung when ships at sea were lost or in trouble. That still happens and entries are made in a log book with a quill pen as they always have been, so we were told.

No riotous living took place while Derek was not with us. We greatly missed him and I still hate shorthand-typing. That is just my own pet hate occupation. I do have a great admiration for those who do it so well daily and are wonderful secretaries. Fortunately I still can type, otherwise this story might not have been told.

John and Ken Ling with Derek and Granddad Beaven

We visited Derek frequently and he often came home. According to his reports he was doing well but once again a move was approaching and off we went to Stevenage in Hertfordshire. This was before the building of the New Town. Working at deHavillands now, Cliff was sent often on business to La Jolla, California, and to Australia on weapons research work.

Whether it was his own strong desire that we should go and live in Australia, or deHavillands who suggested it, I do not know but today I have my suspicions. We were both young and ready to do anything and go anywhere together but I was not happy at disturbing Derek so often. Bless him, he was so good and eager for a new experience in another part of the world. As for me, I had not minded our previous moves; after all, my parents had moved me four times already before I was married and I could cope with comments from folk who said,

"We need new address books because of you".

Australia and Afterwards

Our passage to Australia on board SS Iberia - 1958

Derek is now an established author and in his second novel he writes an account of a sea journey which I recognise as being similar to our own. We sailed from Tilbury in December 1958 on the SS Iberia, first class, courtesy of deHavilland. A five week journey and a really wonderful experience. We had left England, our relations and friends and had no idea when we might see them again. I fear that we had not thought how hard it must have seemed for our close relatives as they waved goodbye from the dock.

There were several scheduled stops on the way, notably Gibraltar, although having arrived there at midnight, delayed by fog in the English Channel, we could see nothing. At Suez we had a two-day wait for a passage through the canal. It was not long after the Suez troubles during Anthony Eden's government, giving a few local Egyptians excuse to crudely show their disdain.

We disembarked at Aden but Bombay (Mumbai) had to be missed. At Colombo, Ceylon (Sri Lanka) we were taken by some new friends to their home and delightfully entertained as guests. Singapore was a fascinating, highly populated country. We were there for a few days and bought ourselves cameras, a Yashica which I still have, and a cine camera.

Photo slides were popular then; armed with a screen and projector you could entertain or bore your audience for hours. We were dismayed, though, by the disgustingly haughty behaviour of British settlers towards the local people. Perth, Western Australia, was our first stop on the Australian continent and we had a pleasant time in and around that beautiful city.

Adelaide, South Australia, was our destination and Cliff's new job was to be with EMI for some connection with deHavillands. We were found accommodation, not in the outback although I think Cliff did have to visit Woomera. Derek became a founder-member of a new local school where, unfortunately, he suffered a broken arm playing Rugby. I had a short stay in hospital for an operation on both wrists to clear a pins-and-needles condition in my fingers.

For fifteen months we lived Down Under. Some things were good; sunshine was abundant and temperatures of 100/110 C not exceptional but it was a dry heat, not humid as in Sydney. When it rained we stood in the doorway and filmed scenes for proof. One could get quite rich then as the taxman sometimes refunded money and provisions were cheaper than in the UK. Of course, if taxes are low you get poor roads, etc. We bought ourselves a new Holden Hatchback car and in the holidays made a round trip to Melbourne, Sydney (this was before the opera house was built) and inland through WaggaWagga to Canberra, which was all very interesting.

However, things did not go well at work for Clifford. The position to which he was sent was found not to be vacant, or maybe whoever occupied it was not willing to vacate. The alternative given was that we could be flown back to England if we wished. In the spring of 1960 we flew back on a Comet airplane and on arrival were accommodated at RAF Lyneham, noticing an abrupt drop in temperature but being well warmed and cared for. We were virtually homeless but after a few weeks of temporary addresses, were back in Aylesbury where Clifford was re-employed.

Eventually we settled in a newly-built chalet-style house at Berkhamsted, Herts, and Derek became established at Ashlyns School. I am pleased to announce that we stayed in that house for nine years, the longest anywhere so far. Derek had survived all the changes. Ashlyns was a good, active school and he made his mark, as he always did and as we knew he would.

In the sixth form he became Head Boy and in due course, on his Latin performance won a scholarship to St Peter's College, Oxford University. Between our house and the town ran the Grand Union Canal and parallel to it, the

London to North West railway line. The latter was being electrified while we lived there and the Great Train Robbery took place only a few miles along the line.

Our lives were full of incident. Most memorably we were there for the extremely cold winter which started on Boxing Day 26/12/1962. Everywhere was frozen for three months; we had a direct line to town by walking under the railway bridge then straight across the canal on the solid ice, or on the immovable lock gates, until an icebreaking vessel was sent through in March 1963. This cold winter I believe was worse than the one in 1946/7, when I was pregnant with Derek. That was followed by one of our hottest summers.

As soon as we were in our new house, Clifford was changing jobs again. He wished to be back at Imperial College but was willing to do the daily journeys to and from London. Adjoining the college in Prince Consort Road and a faculty of it is The Royal School of Mines and his work would now involve lecturing, so far as I knew in Physics, Electrical Engineering and computerisation as applied to open-cast mining of minerals. This connected with the work he had done on early computers at Air

Trainers, so it seemed a good and profitable situation at last and he was happy.

He had done several business trips abroad with deHavilland colleagues but at College specialists were given a set financial allowance for trips. Wives were not specifically paid for but were welcome to go along on this same allowance. Indeed wives were expected to be involved and an asset (and do much of the driving), so several Augusts were spent in other countries. It was always enjoyable but frequently exhausting. Whilst in London for the rest of the year I was a member of the College Wives' Club, our work largely being to welcome and entertain business visitors from abroad and their wives and to be present at social occasions. It was a great life, in the heart of London.

Soon after we returned to England in 1960, Cliff wanted me to try for membership of the Institute of Advanced Motorists, which I did. I had been driving since I was 22. I passed their test. I have always enjoyed driving and still do. It is dangerous to boast about the achievement as that might lead to a crash, but it certainly gave me skill and confidence which have been invaluable in my years of driving throughout the world.

 I remained a member for nearly 45 years, only ceasing when my previous car really died of exhaustion. For 18 months I was without my own vehicle but life was so difficult that I became a driver again. If you are asking the obvious question, yes, I know how to cope with a less than perfect arm on the steering wheel.

Gathering Momentum

From the 1960s through to the 70s, life seems to have been rushing on to a climax, which indeed it was. Most of the old aunts and uncles in our families had died, Cliff had started on journeys abroad for College and Derek and I joined in the trip through Belgium and Holland as our planned holiday.

We were en route to Sweden, to silver and copper mines not quite so far north as the university town of Uppsala. I know we explored Stockholm, enjoyed hospitality from friends and colleagues, found Sweden very clean and tidy and brought home some Orrefors glass but have no other clear memories. On returning, Derek wished to make his way home alone through France and he sent us a postcard from Avignon.

Our family now had increased to include Jane Sheard, Derek's friend of Ashlyns school days. They both finished their university days, Jane at Holloway College, and then were married at Berkhamsted Church, much to our pleasure. We loved Jane and welcomed her.

L-R back brother Ronald, Kenneth and John Ling, Clifford. Front: Cliff's mum, Noreen, my mother, Derek, Jane and me

Kenneth and John Ling at Derek and Jane's Wedding

George Ling and Derek

I know exactly where I was when the US President, John F. Kennedy was shot; we were watching the 6 o'clock news at home in Berkhamsted. It was the biggest terrible political event that we had seen on television, certainly in great contrast to the happier occasion of Queen Elizabeth II's coronation in 1953 which had shown the world something of what television could do at that time. There is no shortage of sad and happy big events today; we saw Sir Edmund Hillary and Tensing Norgay reach the top of Mount Everest, we have watched the first man walk on the moon and even the ghastly events in New York on 11th September 2001, the Aberfan colliery disaster in Wales in October 1966, the IRA bombings, wars all over the world, famines and the distress of those who suffer. Not wanting to give a sermon here, for which I am certainly not qualified, I will just say that it has all been part of my life.

A memorable August college trip was to the USA in 1966. In five weeks, Cliff and I travelled over five thousand miles around the States. Sadly I kept no diary but we left London Heathrow by BOAC to New York and were met by English friends Gwen and David Southgate who had left England to make their home there.

Before us lay a round trip to various opencast mining operations, ending with a conference at Milwaukee. At Cleveland, Ohio, we were welcomed by my cousin Doris, sister to Gordon, Joyce and Ruby Main, and Doris's husband Angelo. Doris had come to America as a GI Bride. Seeing her is a happy memory; we had been children together and she was much missed. Sadly Doris died of cancer a few years later.

Our high spots on this trip included Oklahoma City, Arizona, New Mexico, Denver City, Colorado, the Grand Canyon where we stayed for a weekend, Salt Lake City and Chicago. While we were away we were sent news that my father had died but as we were committed to the workload I was unable to return at that point. I wish I felt sad about that; in childhood I had thought well of him and loved him, as one does. As I entered my teens, though, I knew there was an uncomfortable feeling between us and now every thought of him brings me to anger. Of course he was a man with normal needs, but not me! I am your DAUGHTER!! But I am pleased to remember that when the England footballers won the World Cup that year Dad had watched that on television and it would have been a great thrill for him.

You may think I had left music behind, but not so, as at this time I had the opportunity to make headway. It is necessary to recall wartime days when, living at Thornton Heath and earning money at my war work, I first decided that as I could not hope to become a professional piano soloist I could at least sing. So I went to Miss Irene Burr and asked for some lessons. She was very pleased that I did but asked why I had not been sent to her for piano tuition. I think I must have been with her about eighteen months but, sadly for me, she was about to retire and live with her brother in Devon.

She was not a voice specialist but she did set me on the right path. Instantly she recognised my musical abilities and thought I should sing, first for experience, with the Croydon Philharmonic Society. "Aim high, Freda," She said. So I applied, was auditioned and accepted. This meant one evening each week for rehearsal and then concerts; some in Croydon and many thereafter in London, often at the Royal Albert Hall joining BBC Choirs and other big London choirs. We worked on home ground under the direction of Alan J Kirby, a great Elgar enthusiast, performing Elgar works frequently but not solely. Ralph Vaughan Williams conducted us on one occasion and we sang a Mass of Life by Delius at the Davis Theatre, Croydon, conducted by Sir Thomas Beecham.

When I married I was still singing with the Croydon Phil. Clifford did not object but never showed any interest, so I aimed higher and by the time we had left Berkhamsted and moved to Ham near Richmond, I had auditioned for and joined the BBC Symphony Chorus. This was amateur choir work of a very high standard and eventually I was accepted by John McCarthy for the Ambrosian Singers, professionals doing session work. My time with them was brief due to circumstances at home, but I did achieve that status and performed with them several times.

There was so much to enjoy in the busy London musical world wherein I found myself, and now I could be in London, sometimes with Cliff at College and on journeys of my own.

With Clifford and Derek both away all day, I studied every day at home for two years to gain theoretical knowledge and to voice train, with a qualified local teacher, and reached the standard – and beyond because it interested me – for LRAM written paper work. Clifford was in agreement that I should follow this path. Then having moved nearer to college and central London, he had an easier daily journey and I was nearer to my activities. Wishing to do some serious voice work, I contacted Professor Henry Cummings FRAM and took external (to the academy) voice training with him. With Henry and Norah Newby his wife and brilliant accompanist I studied the wonderful repertoires of English, French, Italian and German Song for three years.

Later, Betty Bannerman, a fine French Song specialist, was my mentor and I had two lessons with the great Pierre Bernac. I love to sing in all these languages and indeed, they have been the basis of my teaching career. In 1967 I sat and gained the LRAM Teacher's Diploma and the following year achieved the higher Performer's Diploma. These exams took place at the Royal Academy of Music in Marylebone Road, together with academy students.

I love music of many kinds. It surely was no crime to improve my understanding of a subject. It has been the means of keeping me alive and if life were longer I would probably become a musicologist. Music stirs me, arouses, feeds and soothes all my emotions, fulfils my needs and tests my brain.

I record all these details because it was the path I trod to become a qualified musician. It was a fight but I have had to fight all my life. I guess we all do if we want to move on, one way or another. It would have been pleasant to have heard a "well done" or "I'm proud of you", once in a while but those are not the kind of comments I received. Of course I know that I am first, last and always a wife and mother and am proud to be so, but there were all those days to fill. Was it so wrong to live my life? My family was never neglected; I managed to run our home with plenty of tender loving care but I had to do things for myself.

When a man changes a job he immediately has colleagues but his wife is left to find her own occupation in each new place. For me, after qualifying, that has meant finding pupils, which takes time, then having to depart and find another group. A social life is important too. It may sound as though music and the gaining of diplomas were all just to be a clever girl. In fact music itself is a treasure which comes first on any list of mine but I have many other interests which all contribute to fulfilment in life. Music has been the main source of income from all the teaching I've done since 1967 and indeed has kept me alive with a roof over my head. This necessity, although I did not know it, was not far ahead.

Towards the end of the sixties Derek and Jane had not found anywhere particularly pleasing to live and the suggestion was made that, if we looked outside London we might find somewhere that would suit us all together, although in separate accommodation. We looked long and carefully and eventually found an Old School Cottage in Hampshire. Some work had been done for conversion to living quarters and all four of us continued the project. It was enormously hard work but they were young and we were still fit. Finally we had two separate dwellings, one in each end of the building. Cliff's parents, Noreen and George with their two sons John and Kenneth all visited, as did friends and colleagues.

In 1971 another five-week college trip arose, taking Cliff and me to Rhodesia (Zimbabwe) and South Africa. This was at the time when apartheid was the norm and we found a highly sensitive political situation. We went with no intention of being political but it was thrust upon us in various situations, making the visit frighteningly unpleasant. Yes, we visited Victoria Falls, copper and diamond mines, had wonderful weekends at Game Parks seeing all the big five wildlife at Mala-Mala, but were glad to be in the air for the return journey and arrived home with very gloomy faces.

My mother had not been well after my father died. Ron and Olive had managed to help her settle into a nursing home at South Croydon after she had left her house. I had always lived many miles away from home and now, when she was ill and needed attention and company, there were 70 miles between us. We were used to long car journeys. Cliff's parents' home was at Abbey Wood, right across London, and we agreed that neither of us ought to do 70-miles driving alone.

Since that time I have covered many more miles alone. Times have changed and with my mother in need it was not long before that rule had to be dropped and I made weekly visits to her so that we could have afternoon tea somewhere in the countryside and perhaps buy her a new dress and whatever she needed. Sometimes we went to Shirley Hills. She kept all her faculties into her 81st year but died eventually in February 1972. During her last few years friends and relations had visited Mother, in particular my late cousin Joyce who often was with her near the end, for which I am most grateful.

Ten days later Olive phoned me to tell me that my brother Ron had died. He had taken his car for the first time into a car-wash facility, saying "It will be a new experience" and he was noticed to be collapsed at the wheel. He was taken to hospital but after two days had not regained consciousness. All that smoking which he had learned so long ago had taken its toll and his heart could no longer work. He was 56 years old. These days he probably would have been operated upon and saved – a frequent cry upon someone's death.

Ron was a gifted pianist and organist, artist in oils – his work had been chosen for exhibition in a London military services exhibition - had moved from Croydon with his wife Olive and their two adopted children Paul and Irene to the Malvern area because of his love of Elgar's music and that part of the country. We did not always see eye to eye; he had become a Roman Catholic and I would have liked to have known him in our later lives and shared some earlier thoughts and memories with him. Our relationship was not a bad or unpleasant one, as some might make out.

Mother's twin, Grace had died during the early 1960s at Croydon and I remember that after the funeral Mother went upstairs to bed and remained there silently, undisturbed, for an hour or so. After that I never heard her speak again of Grace for the rest of her life. How strange.

Near the end of her life Mother had told me that she wanted to leave her body to medical science and asked me to arrange that. She had no sisters alive and foresaw only a low attendance at her funeral. I think she was mistaken in that point as she still had lifelong friends and her nieces and nephews would have come to say goodbye to their Auntie Anne, but I did as she asked. None of the family wrote or contacted me but I had a kind letter from one of her friends. Today the world is vastly different; we are more spread about, have cars, telephones and modern miraculous equipment which makes today's children think we lived in the Dark Ages.

It was when we had thought ourselves more or less comfortably settled in our double house that the thunderbolt struck. Jane said that it was nothing to do with our being at close quarters and I think she was right. We should have been able to help each other but in fact both our marriages were breaking up. For two years Cliff and I had been seeking help from our doctor and a psychiatrist, both of us together and separately, as we were certainly not running smoothly. I had always thought that we were happily married and that by seeking help we could avoid bringing distress to our immediate families and be guided to a happier situation ourselves.

Part of the problem, I guess, was that I had been in demand amongst the local musical circle as soon as we moved there. The Music Festival wanted me on their committee, pupils arrived, I was invited to give a song recital and also requested to be musical director of an existing madrigal group. For four years I ran this group successfully as an evening class in Further Education and we gave much-praised concerts. I was booked to sing Handel's "Silete Venti" with Peter Marhbank's orchestra and we gave a repeat performance at the Lord Penney theatre in Harwell. Lord Penney was at that time Head of Imperial College and I knew his wife, Lady Penney, from our Wives' Club connection. Then Reading University offered me a teaching post and twice tried hard to get me. I could not be persuaded as I had a husband to look after.

Still happily involved with Cliff's work and friends at college, and keeping house, I managed to fit in all of this. I have long realised that what I enjoy so much is not everybody's pleasure, but it is what I do and has given me a wide circle of friends of like thinking which has been very valuable. Never have I expected oceans of praise but I would have appreciated just some respect for music itself, for what I do and courtesy to my musical friends. Was I supposed to push all this activity out of my life? It was just acceptable that I could 'play the piano' but to go further seems to have been beyond the pale. Clifford showed no interest and would not attend any of my musical occasions. It was not within his subject – Physics, which, he believed, taught him *everything*. He had done well to get to Imperial College as a student, gained a BSc degree, became a member of the Institute of Electrical Engineers and of MENSA, and was widely experienced in his career.

We were, however, deeply distressed. One night in 1974, I had collected him from the railway station as usual. As we ate our meal he told me he was about to sign an agreement at college whereby he would go to work in Sudan for three years. I said "Sudan? I don't think I want to go to live there". Cliff said "I didn't think you would".

So his idea of mending our marriage was to go away for three years. Well, that was it. If he could walk away, so could I. What else was I supposed to do? Stay alone in our four-part agreement home? I don't think so.

From South to North

So that was our family disintegration and very painful it was. One of those pains which pass into life's background but never disappear. Inevitably what I have written has been much about me as it is my life story that I wish to tell, but that does not mean that there has been no thought-sharing concerning my nearest and dearest. When Derek came to tell us he and Jane were separating they had been married for four years, Cliff and I for twenty-nine. Upon taking the step of sharing a property our solicitor advised us each to sign a four-part agreement on the shared financial value of our homes. A wise precaution, as when it did become necessary to sell we were all due a share. Jane valiantly declined to sign until my signature was obtained.

Since our parting I have not spread wild accusations about my husband, only stated what has happened. We had loved each other steadfastly and perhaps both tried to keep the peace when differences arose. We did not scream and shout but I believe we should have done a bit of that sometimes and not kept upsets to ourselves. Word has come back to me that latterly I did not respond kindly to any suggestions he made. Remembering how throughout our life together his ideas had so often led to a change of job, a change of abode – even to the ends of the earth – and finally that he should use dynamite to blow up some concrete right outside our kitchen window, perhaps by now I could be excused for some lack of enthusiasm. A word or two, such as "I am pleased you enjoy your music" or "I am proud of you" or "I'd love to meet your musical friends" could have made a world of difference but that never happened. We were just not on the same wave-length. When we first were in love I told him I would go to the moon with him if he wished, and I would have done. His occupation then was posing that as a real, if remote possibility.

I did not fall on my feet, as has been assumed, but into floods of tears and deep despair. Did people think that my marriage being split and my family spread far and wide meant nothing to me? Their thoughts were for 'poor Cliff'; what about 'poor Freda'?

Once, long ago, my mother-in-law, upon seeing I had been weeping, said "We don't often see YOU crying!" Do I present a hide like a rhinoceros? But a roof to lie under had to be found and a job of work to provide essential money. My recent earnings from private teaching (£150) I took with me and Derek took me, with a few possessions, in our Toyota, registered in my name but I wanted him to take it back to his father, to my new address in Marple, Cheshire. I had left my beloved south of England to go northwards. It was early in January. 1975. I could have gone anywhere but Chester friends Jenny and David Sims had suggested I went near to them. Jenny had been a voice pupil of mine and sang in my madrigal group.

My new abode had been a doctor's residence and was now divided into bedsits with shared use of bathroom and kitchen. The room was large, clean and pleasant, close to shops and trains to Manchester. I don't know how I coped for the first few weeks, it is now all a blur, but I do remember that tears flowed freely. Grief, they say, like graveyard earth, takes time to settle. I wrote to a few folk back home and after a week or two some replies began to arrive. One from Clifford saying he had been ill and he hoped I was all right. He had left the house before I did.

Another came from Aunt Ethel Goldsmith, the gist of which was "poor Cliff". Best of all was such a kind letter from my friend Lorna in Gloucester, and indeed her unending love and understanding have been the greatest help to me to this day. Derek was wonderful and supportive and continued to be for many years. Why did I go north? I have often asked myself. Manchester appealed as a musical area, I knew Jenny and David and also I knew a man on friendly terms, who had helped me to find the Marple flat and we remained friends, on and off, for many years. I wrote to Clifford's mother but received no reply, to Noreen and George and did receive a kind and loving letter

The first step forward was to find an employment agency in Manchester. The only thing I could offer that could bring good enough money was shorthand-typing. Much to my surprise there was a job just waiting for me so I found my way along about a mile to Ardwick Green for an interview. There were two gentlemen running their own businesses together. Mr Kelsey dealt in textiles, not surprisingly, Manchester having been cotton king around here, and Mr Wilkinson handled leather for the bookbinding trade.

In addition to doing their letters I dealt with the money and the bookkeeping ledgers, the telephone switchboard and providing lunch for the two men. This meant buying what they wanted to eat, as I went to the bank each day, and preparing the food in the back kitchen. Head Cook and Bottlewasher really but it was not unpleasant. They liked bacon butties (being a soft southerner I had to learn what butties were), fish cakes, followed by chocolate cupcakes or biscuits, strawberries and cream in the summer. My biggest problem was the switchboard. Not being a natural lover of telephones (two good hands would be a help) I had to get used to the deep-voiced northern-speaking customers who would run through their requirements at speed while I tried to decipher what they were saying. My circle of acquaintances expanded as their sales staff appeared at the office through the weeks and upstairs was another member of the firm called Alec. He was not far off retirement, a kindly man with whom I had many chats.

This was deep winter in Manchester. It was not always raining but it was dismal and colder than the south by about ten degrees. A new winter coat was a necessity so I sold my engagement ring – not a good experience. We had been so happy in December 1944 and full of plans for the future but reality had stepped in and dismissed sentimentality. One thing I soon noticed was that in the north building bricks were a dull red, not the bright cheerier red of the south. I don't think this was industrial deposit but just that the bricks are a darker shade. Using buses posed a problem to a newcomer as information about their destinations was scarce, virtually non-existent. Today Manchester is a very modern city.

So now I had a roof, a job and an income. I was occupied and lived from day to day in my one room. After a few months our house was sold and my share of the proceeds duly arrived, enabling me to buy a car. What bliss to be mobile again! One evening I went to a concert at the Royal Northern College of Music, got talking to the person next to me and discovered she was a pianist/accompanist and music teacher and she offered me a studio in her house at Northwich in Cheshire. That would mean I could start teaching again, evenings after work. My employers didn't need to know this, they might have thought I would get too exhausted to work for them.

It was hard but I survived and began to be known in the district. A circle of musical professionals was beginning to develop and for pleasure I sang with some pro SATB choralists, sometimes in Manchester cathedral. Music seemed to be awaiting me there, and wherever I have lived I have quickly found myself musically known and appreciated. In 1979 I was admitted to membership of The Royal Society of Musicians of Great Britain.

For two-and-a-half years, my life was centred on my two gentlemen in Ardwick Green and eventually the chance occurred for me to move to a flat in North Manchester owned by a housing corporation. Not having many pieces of furniture I managed to transfer what I had to the flat by making several car journeys with filled cardboard cartons. The weather was bitterly cold. I moved in on a Saturday but could not have electricity until the following Monday. Nature caught up with me and quickly laid me low with real influenza. Fortunately I had landed amongst very kind neighbours who called a doctor and cared for me.

A great joy in 1979 was Derek's marriage to Winnie Sidhu and in due course the arrival of my granddaughter, Kirstie Anna, and later my grandson, Jonathan Francis Seymour. In September 2010 Kirstie married Luke Youngman, and now I have two gorgeous great-grandchildren, Blythe Daisy and Hal Peter. We are all in touch on social media.

Derek with Winnie and her mother at their wedding.

Through all my experience in forty-two years of living in the north of England I have met so many kind people, many of whom I still know today. I would not like to risk missing out anybody by naming these friends but I will never forget them. Also for pure enjoyment I have motored around Lancashire, Yorkshire, Cumbria and into Scotland; the beauty all around soothes me and brings great peace of mind. Driving southwards frequently to London, Hampton, Maidenhead, Winchester, Gloucester and sometimes to the south coast gives assurance that both the south and the north are now my homes.

But I am not a northerner; there are differences but they do not matter. Sometimes with maybe half-an-hour to spare between pupils, I sit in my car beside the sea (actually the mouth of the River Mersey) by the coastguard station and just absorb the scene; high tide or low, river traffic large and small, people with their dogs on the sands, soaring flocks of birds, and enjoy the perfection of the sweeping horizon.

From January 1980, for the next eight years, having left my job at Ardwick, the top-of-the-Pennines town of Oldham became my life centre. At school we had known about the backbone of England called The Pennine Hills and it had interested me. I had no idea that I would live and work there.

Colleagues David Butterworth, Annice Roy, Eileen Bentley and Freda at her Bury house.

My new job was as a peripatetic music teacher going into six or seven schools each week to organise and lead children's choirs. How those children sang for me! We worked to a high standard of ability and enjoyment. Employed at Oldham Metropolitan Music Centre, I was one of three specialist voice teachers there and accompanist to some of the groups. Also I was in charge of the Theory of Music department – very much my speciality. After school hours many pupils attended at the Centre to work in groups of strings, brass and woodwind as well as choirs and to have individual tuition, so we tutors were on duty usually till 9pm.

Dobcross School children in Victorian dress for musical drama production

Many trips out took various groups to compete at music festivals and to do overseas tours. Over one thousand children each week attended the evening sessions, with invaluable transportation help from their parents. It thrived for many years under the direction of Dr Eileen Bentley MBE, a very dear friend of mine of many years' standing.

My work at Oldham also extended to the local Technical College where I gave individual and group voice tuition to students on a three-year Performing Arts Course. Years of studying, performing and teaching German Lieder, French and Italian Song had polished my languages so I was able to give speech coaching and language tuition to students, some of whom I now see established in radio and television work.

Oldham is situated at almost the highest point of the Pennines and the climate is often known to be an overcoat colder than Manchester. I found the winters taxing and dangerously slippery underfoot. Time was marching on. The colleagues and friends with whom I worked made it a pleasure to be there where I was respected and my work considered of value. We had great social fun too.

Now into the 1980s it became possible for me to buy a property, and for this I thank the Thatcher government. As I had paid a monthly rental on my housing corporation flat for nine years the government would refund me my payments and enable me to become a house-owner, if I so chose. I could buy anywhere. In 1975 this would not have been possible but it was now an exciting prospect. After a recession, banks could lend again and I was able to get a mortgage. In blind faith, thinking I could teach music to the end of my days (of course I can) I went ahead and after much searching, consulting and deliberating bought a charming stone cottage just outside Bury in Lancashire, where I lived for the next five years.

My years at Oldham had been a truly golden time, remembered with deep affection and emotion. Completely involved in music, there were few longings for the past, with the exception of family conversation. Scientific matters are of interest to me and I miss talk of the kind we used to have. But I am widely read in many subjects and keep myself up-to-date by radio, television and all I can lay hands upon. The present is reality.

My retirement from Rushcroft School 1988

Picture Gallery 2

Winnie, Kirstie Freda and Luke – 2012

Jonathan in confident mood and in his pyjamas - 1990

Klaus and Margrit Brinkmann – c.2005

Kirstie and Luke Youngman at Freda's home

Winnie – mother of the bride at the marriage of Luke and Kirstie – 2010

My beloved Becky Tallentire

Margaret Ryman, my friend and neighbour of the last 27 years

Christmas Day at Edith Maggs' house with Tony Johnson

Jean Dobson – AOTOS friend

Cecilia, Ruth, Freda and Constance – AOTOS friends 1980s

With Hazel, Joyce's daughter

Barbara Simpson - past pupil and lunch and theatre companion

The Austrian Holiday

Berwang, Austria

In the late 1950s while Clifford, Derek and I were having our Australian experience, two people were driving through the Austrian Tyrol area and came upon a delightful small village high up in the mountains. They stayed for a few days and were captivated by the beauty of the scenery, the tranquillity and the friendliness of the people. The brilliant idea came to them that this would be an ideal place to run a holiday music course.

Upon returning to their London home, they pursued the matter and in due course the Berwang Holiday Music Course came into being. The travellers were Henry

Cummings and his wife Norah Newby. Henry was then Head of Voice Studies at the Royal Academy of Music and Norah was Pianist/Accompanist, also at the Academy. The course became well established and is still enthusiastically running.

Henry and Norah Cummings who started it all.

The structure is that each group (strings, woodwind, brass and singers) rehearses for two sessions on Monday, Tuesday is a holiday, Wednesday is a work day etc., with possible weather adjustments, all aiming to come together to give two main concerts during the two-week stay. Each group is led by a professional musician, most of the players being visitors of acceptable musical standard and/or experience, who want a holiday exactly on those lines. People come from all over the world, mostly from Britain and some are students from the colleges. Listeners are welcome.

I was studying with Professor Henry Cummings in the 1960s and he came to our house overnight once when he was adjudicating at Basingstoke and suggested we went to Berwang on this holiday course. Cliff and I shared the driving en route through Belgium, France, Germany and over the border at Ottobeuren into the Austrian Tyrol.

In the hot August weather we enjoyed ourselves and joined a large group of players and listeners who were housed in various hotels and guest houses in the village. On non-working days we went on coach trips to Linderhof and Neuschwanstein castles, Salzburg, Oberammergau, Vienna, Innsbruck and elsewhere.

The village had a heated open air swimming pool and there were woodland and mountain walks for local day trips and chair lifts to the top of ski runs. The local cafes excelled themselves with delicious drinks, coffee and Black Forest gateaux. Listeners on the course, of whom there would be several, were of varied professions and interests, could attend any work sessions or were free to do whatever they wished for the music hours.

Clifford came for a second year and we took with us a friend named Ann, but it seems that he was not mixing very well and was overwhelmed by the proximity of so many people who understood and enjoyed music. The next year he suggested I went alone, which suited us both.

Later, when I was working for Oldham Education Committee, they allowed me to go on the music holiday as an extension to my professional work for them, and they paid for me from 1980 until I retired in 1988. Since that time I have had to fund myself from my state pension and private teaching and I made sure to go to Austria whenever possible, and often on the same trip to visit dear friends in Holland whom I have known them since our Aylesbury days and who have been a wonderful joy in my life. Berwang is a wonderful place for music. There I have worked and holidayed with people who love me and appreciate what I do. Music of various kinds flows all around us and from us. In 2007 I had reached my twentieth visit and received a charming brooch from the Austrian tourist Board, and a wonderful ovation.

Workers in the Voice Section

The Strings and Wind section

Full rehearsal

For a few years I gave song classes at Berwang which were much enjoyed. In addition to our two main concerts for the local public we entertained ourselves on some evenings with informal concerts. When my brother Ron died, I found and rescued some songs which he had written. They were settings of poems, one by James Stephens *The Daisies*, Gerard Manley Hopkins' *Heaven Haven* and *Love is a Sickness* by Samuel Daniel. Not a song cycle but a collection. I just wrote them out in good style, published, and performed them at Berwang to great acclamation. One comment was that the aura of those times just floated around the room. Ron had written a song for me as a birthday present and I sang that and wished he was there to hear. Though I am not a believer in the supernatural I had the queer feeling that he touched me on my shoulder afterwards.

I should explain that often I have met the accusation that singers are not musicians. This is obviously true for many singers; you don't have to be a musician to sing, but many of us are certainly fully qualified and experienced in our profession.

The year 2008 had to be my last visit to Berwang as old age creeps on apace, making travel abroad quite difficult. Airports are for the young, especially these days with active terrorism likely, insurance nearly impossible for one of my age with angina and because I can no longer climb the steep hills of the village. But it was a wonderful time of my life and many friends are still in touch.

Jill Robinson

Freda with two handsome men: Kerry and Simon

Anne Harcombe

Joan White with her beloved Ben

Drinks with Jean Dolan

www.musicholiday.com

Retirement

Freda and her loyal old friend of 50 years, the Bechstein

In times gone by, retirement meant stopping work and enjoying or not enjoying the rest of life. Now a communications revolution is taking place and many of my generation find occupations for lively minds and relatively agile bodies.

Those of us who survived the 1939-45 war and the following years of getting our country back on its feet find our retirement age challenging, to say the least. We don't know how we found time to go to work, and if we are fortunate, have interests in abundance and time for relaxation. Old age does take its toll, however, and our bodies tell us of each new restriction.

When I was 65 and newly retired from college employment, life began again in a different style. I left Oldham but there was still a call for me to return (a) to discuss my work with teachers from schools in which I had worked, so that they could continue in my footsteps and keep singing alive in their classes, and (b) I had a tutoring practice there running all day Saturdays for private pupils and so travelled between home and Oldham for several years. There was no way I could have sat back and stopped working – a mortgage had still to be paid and the wolf kept from the door. In fact, a new mortgage, as there had been yet another change of address.

Whilst still living at Bury I was invited by a friend, Jill Robinson, whom I had met on the Austrian holiday, to visit her and her family in Geneva for a welcome break. Jill's two daughters were working for the Associated Board of the Royal Schools of Music theory exams and they asked my help. Jill suggested I should write a theory text book showing the way I taught the subject. So, back at home I started to do so. It was a monumental task but I greatly enjoyed myself. The book finally became 287 pages long and I started my own desktop registered publishing company named *Roselle Publications*.

I travelled around Lancashire and Yorkshire selling copies to music shops, getting it circulated, and together with mail orders sold around 900 copies in the UK and abroad. Entitled *Music Theory Makes Sense*, it is still much in use today. Selling the first batch paid for a reprint but after the second reprint the money ran out. The ABRSM were just issuing a re-working of their own theory books so I was in direct competition.

Another occupation at that time was adjudicating for the British Federation of Music Festivals for several years and odd sessions of examining which came my way. Adjudicating is hard and responsible work, with long hours for big classes but often a great pleasure. It meant much travel and weekends away from home but it paid well and I met many colleagues along the way.

At one festival I was on the Saturday night adjudicating panel with the late Norman Tattersall, who asked me to apply for membership of the Association of Teachers of Singing (www.aotos.org.uk) of which he had been a founder member. I did so and became a member of this prestigious body. Members are from the ranks of Academy and College tutors, together with private voice specialist teachers from all over Britain, all being experienced professional musicians. We meet several times each year in conference and enjoy meeting our colleagues, exchanging teaching experiences, learning and singing together, making our individual contributions, having master classes, discussions and social gatherings.

The art of singing requires much psychological, physiological and technical knowledge to link the voice with words and music and to communicate to the world. In other words, to show us what is on the page. In 2007 I was made an Emeritus Member of AOTOS.

Bury had been my home for five years since 1985. My stone cottage had a small area backed by an eight-foot high stone wall where I had made a little garden. Pupils came for piano, musicianship and singing lessons and many friends came.

Surrounded by hills and moors and having a fine market hall where I bought lengths of fabric for dressmaking, the town was pleasant but a touch cold in winter. Ada, a long-established stallholder, always produced something choice but there seemed little for me to join in with otherwise. I had a flautist friend, Joan Simpkin, there and thought I might consider a change, so by the end of February my Bury house was sold and I removed again, to the northwest coast, with a new mortgage to support.

That is now 27 years ago and I sincerely hope this twenty-second address will be my last. We don't see much of the sea as shifting sands over the years have made it stay away, but it does reach the sea walls on very high tides. A fine boating lake is much in use and our main thoroughfare is a mile long and one of the widest and most beautiful streets in the country, full of listed buildings.

I did run into a web of problems here, firstly a legal problem over house maintenance, a gun held at my back in the local post office, being accosted by fake policemen when driving home one night, and several years of serious drug-related troubles. Now things are settled and I am surrounded by the kindest and most helpful friends and neighbours one could imagine.

There were good things happening throughout all these problems as I found no shortage of interests in this area. The first invitation came to run the music section of a small arts club and then I became interested in watercolour painting at a local Art Club, joining in 1991, and latterly mostly working with acrylic paints.

Soon I became very busy with private music pupils, some working for college or university entrance and eventual careers, others purely for pleasure and festivals. Not having a suitable room or studio, I have almost always travelled out to their homes and this has given the great advantage of the parents being involved and seeing what is going on. That has been enjoyable and created lasting friendships.

For seven years I served as Honorary Representative for the Associated Board of the Royal

Schools of Music, which meant being in charge of their performance exam sessions which I held at the local Sixth Form College, with theory exams at another school. I loved doing that but, with advancing years, left before I failed in any way. We have a thriving Bach Choir of which I was a member for 16 years and chairman for seven of those, performing much beautiful music of the baroque era and of a wider repertoire.

Irene Burr's advice – *Aim High, Freda*, given all those years ago has been invaluable and I think she would be pleased to know it meant so much to me. At my advanced age now I am most comfortable when seated, which keeps me driving (on shorter journeys than in past days), reading, occasional painting, patio gardening, and working counted cross-stitch embroideries, which, when framed, fill much wall space; also enjoying lunches with dear friends, being taken to concerts and following news of past pupils, especially Jennifer Johnston whom I taught for nearly five years and who is now well established in the opera world.

Art Club friends with Freda Alston (front) and Irene Bond (right). Trip to Ilkley 1997

So I have told my story and it has been quite an emotional journey for me; there is not always time or opportunity to be emotional when things happen, but I have, as Alan Bennett may say, used my *voice* and said my say.

But have there been no other men in my life? Apart from my husband whom I had dearly loved, my first conquest – if I may call it that – was when I was in my early teens and the young man slightly older. I must have flashed my eyes at him and he reacted as if a bolt from the blue had descended. Mother had friends who moved away to live a country life in Essex; they had a son who pursued me ardently for many months and said he would wait for me. I didn't really want his attentions and we moved to

Guildford. During the war I did have a soldier boyfriend and carried his photograph for some time. He served in Africa with the Royal Artillery but the affair died a death.

Since living alone, a few male contacts have appeared, and disappeared, mostly because they were much younger than me and had thought me younger than I am. And there have been others in this latter part of my life, who have loved me dearly and that I have appreciated, but ways ahead had not been clear.

Obviously I am much better ploughing my way alone and have managed that fairly successfully. I have been able to fulfil my early abilities in music and keep them ongoing, to gather so many friends amongst my pupils and activities, so much care, music, love and laughter which I hope will also abundantly fill the lives of my descendants, who already reach to two gorgeous great-grandchildren.

> So you are here – small being so long hidden from our sight. You look around, when food has lost its urgency, seeing with your mind though your eyes as yet see not.
>
> When were those exquisite eyebrows formed? When came those feet and fingers to perfection?
>
> Long we awaited you – long anticipated – till with sudden determination you arrived, sweet female babe, to contradict our expectations.
>
> All is well: love and comfort abound; you wish to stay, blessing us with queenly dignity. Take from your mother warm food and know that you are welcome.
>
> F.B.

I wrote this on the arrival of my first grandchild in 1979

FREDA BEAVEN © 2017

Printed in Great Britain
by Amazon